Table of Contents

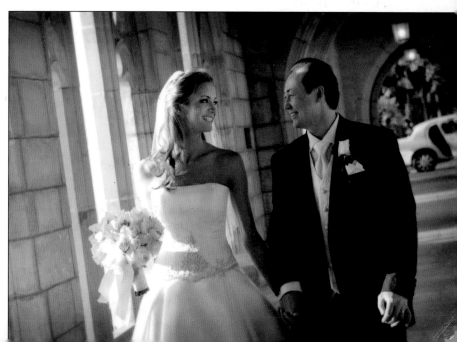

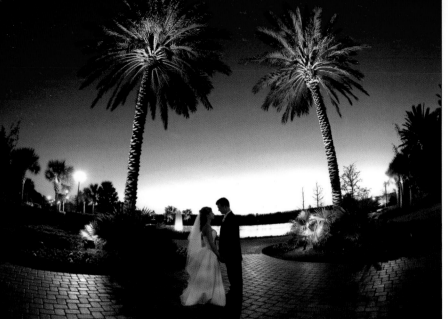

Step-by-Step

WEDDING
PHOTOGRAPHY

TECHNIQUES FOR PROFESSIONAL
PHOTOGRAPHERS

CCI

NY

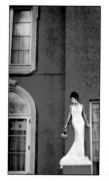

On the front cover—A popular trend recently has been photographing brides against very saturated, colorful backgrounds. (CAMERA: Nikon D2X, ISO: 100, LENS: 17–55mm at 20mm, EXPOSURE: $\frac{1}{200}$ second at f/6.3)

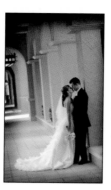

On the back cover—A shot of the couple kissing is always romantic. (CAMERA: Nikon D2Xs, ISO: 400, LENS: 50mm f/1.4, EXPOSURE: $\frac{1}{125}$ second at f/3.5)

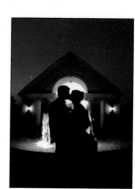

On the back cover—The perfect setting for a nice twilight silhouette. (CAMERA: Nikon D100, ISO: 800, LENS: 16mm, EXPOSURE: $\frac{1}{40}$ second at f/2.8, WHITE BALANCE: tungsten, OTHER: tripod)

ACKNOWLEDGMENTS

Special thanks to my grandmother and father for introducing me to the wonderful world of photography. And to my mother, daughter Tyler, and partner Rosy for all their support. Finally, thanks to all those who have helped me on my artistic journey—there are way too many to list here, but you know who you are.

Published by:
Amherst Media, Inc.
P.O. Box 586
Buffalo, N.Y. 14226
Fax: 716-874-4508
www.AmherstMedia.com

Publisher: Craig Alesse
Senior Editor/Production Manager: Michelle Perkins
Assistant Editor: Barbara A. Lynch-Johnt
Editorial Assistance from: John S. Loder, Carey A. Maines, Charles A. Schweizer

ISBN-13: 978-1-58428-237-2
Library of Congress Control Number: 2008926652
Printed in Korea.
10 9 8 7 6 5 4 3 2 1

About the Author

DAMON TUCCI HAS BEEN A PROFESSIONAL PHOTOGRAPHER for over twenty years. After graduating from Florida State University in 1987 with a degree in filmmaking, Damon signed on as a cinematographer with Glen Lau Productions. One of the world's most famous outdoor photographers and cinematographers, Lau was a legend in the outdoor genre. His Florida-based company produced outdoor adventure and underwater programming for shows such as Sports Afield, Coors Western Outdoorsman, and The American Sportsman. Damon cut his teeth working on Lau's fast-moving projects, learning fabulous lighting tricks and developing a love of 16mm film. While it was great experience, video was rapidly taking over the industry. Damon's 16mm film footage surpassed video in its looks and quality, but it couldn't compete with the lower cost and instant feedback of video.

As this change in the cinematography field was evolving, Damon started shooting Lau's production stills on Fujifilm Velvia slide film with a 35mm Nikon F4 camera. Damon thrived in his new role. Unlike a standard production company where the cameraman is just one cog in the wheel, the still photographer was all on his own. The photo was the end product.

As luck would have it, Walt Disney World was looking for a still photographer for its shows Thunder in Paradise (starring Hulk Hogan) and Star Search. The company hired Damon in 1990, jumpstarting his career as a production still photographer. In addition to the production still work, Damon also started conducting high-end commercial shoots. During his first year at Disney, Damon's assignments ranged from documenting President Bush Sr.'s numerous visits, to shooting restaurant stills for *Food and Wine* magazine, to providing images for company brochures. It was a very exciting year. Every day brought something new.

Then, out of nowhere, the focus changed, and the so-called "Hollywood East" packed up and left. Damon had a choice. Either follow his career to Los

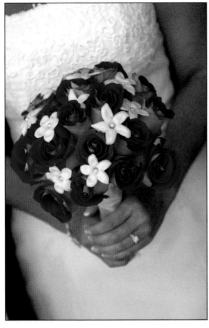

This detail shot of the bride's bouquet was photographed at f/3.5 for a pleasingly shallow depth of field. (CAMERA: Nikon D1X, ISO: 400, LENS: 70–200mm at 70mm, EXPOSURE: $\frac{1}{250}$ second at f/3.5, LIGHTING: available light)

Angeles, or find something new. Around the same time, Walt Disney World opened up Fairytale Weddings. Disney Photographic Services was born to photograph these events under the direction of Steve Powell. Uninspired by the traditional concepts of wedding photography, Damon was initially reluctant to switch his focus from production stills and commercial imagery. However, he took the job and set about trying to spice up his wedding coverage with more avant garde imagery. He was often scolded by his Disney bosses for shooting at odd angles and providing non-traditional images. Damon quickly grew weary of the list of standard shots, such as the bride giving the "OK" sign while holding the wedding certificate on the groom's back, or the tried-and-true shot of the happy couple superimposed inside a champagne flute.

Though he felt punished for pursuing his creative visions, Damon was happy to earn a living with a camera in-hand. His passion for photography helped him make the best of the situation. And it certainly helped to have all the Hasselblads, Nikons, and lighting gear he could ever want at his disposal. Lucky for Damon, brides and grooms evolved their tastes beyond the standard laundry list of shots. They began to seek out the more stylistic, fashion-oriented shots that Damon had always wanted to produce.

Understanding that happy clients mean better revenues, Disney gave Damon more creative freedom, with the only catch that he had to continue to supply the traditional family shots as well. That's when Damon's style was truly born. By 1995, Damon was shooting at least 250 weddings a year, giving him ample opportunity to perfect his mix of fashion and documentary shooting techniques. He quickly learned how to make the contemporary bride and groom happy while also pleasing their more traditionally-minded parents and family.

When Damon left Disney and opened his own studio, he was an extraordinarily experienced photographer for a man his age. As of the writing of this book, Damon has photographed more than 3,500 weddings. Over these thousands of jobs, he has honed his methods to produce consistent results every time. An award-winning photographer who has been featured in numerous bridal and photography magazines, Damon is an eager pioneer in wedding photography techniques who is always willing to share his insights with his fellow professionals.

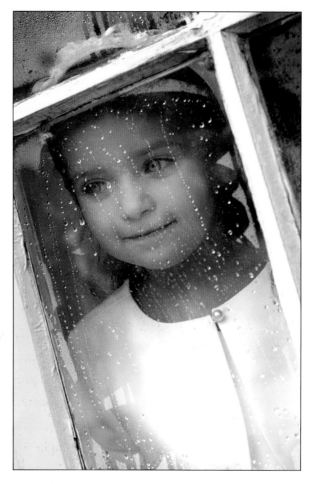

A rain delay set the ceremony a bit behind schedule—but this little girl was full of anticipation. You always have to be on the lookout for these sweet treasures. (CAMERA: Nikon D1X, ISO: 320, LENS: 50mm f/1.4, EXPOSURE: 1/320 second at f/5.0, LIGHTING: available light)

Foreword

*A*T DAMON TUCCI PHOTOGRAPHY, I don't presume to say that my approach is the only way to photograph a wedding, just that it has worked for me and my studio for more than twenty years. Let's face it: Wedding photography is not open-heart surgery, but that doesn't stop someone from suing if you botch one. Do not enter into this profession lightly. The novice photographer should not to put himself in the high-pressure situation of photographing a stranger's wedding without the proper training or experience. A smarter approach is to photograph a friend's wedding from afar—without hindering the hired professional photographer—or volunteer to assist a local pro. In the meantime, you can use this book as a tool to guide you on your path to future success.

OUR STUDIO HAS A NOTICEABLE STYLE THAT COMES FROM OUR SPECIFIC APPROACH TO WEDDING PHOTOGRAPHY.

Style

Our studio has a noticeable style that comes from our specific approach to wedding photography. Essentially, we shoot lean and mean, using a lot of available light. We shoot at a very loose depth of field, typically f/2.8 to f/5.6. When we use flash photography, we use it in combination with ambient light. We strive for a contemporary look, but we pride ourselves on capturing those critical family shots that Mom always asks for.

Learn from the Masters

I've drawn a lot of inspiration from master portrait photographer Michael Glen Taylor. Watching him work on a sunny day in Florida changed the way we shoot on bright days. He walks around almost magically at noon and finds the most amazing pockets of light. He works around the light, sometimes using a reflector, sometimes not. At first glance, there seems to be no method to Michael's uncanny sense of lighting. He just stops and says, "This is it." He then moves the subject into position and makes an exposure.

In Florida, where my studio is located and where we do most of our work, lighting is always a challenge. The natural light is hot and it's always changing. When you're ready for full sun, a cloud drifts overhead. Or it starts to rain. Or you get a mix of the two. It changes often, and it always keeps you on your toes. So a system like Michael's that is fast and flexible works very well.

We've taken knowledge gained from studying these techniques and applied it to the fast-moving world of wedding photography. We love using available light, simplifying our shooting situations where possible, and seeking out pockets of great light. As we learned from Michael, those pockets are everywhere—you just have to train yourself to see them. This is a more involved process than noticing great landscapes or aesthetic scenes. It's a mindful process of observing your environment and how the light falls within it.

Set Goals and Get Inspired

Henry David Thoreau said, "In the long run we only hit what we aim at." In other words, it is good to have goals.

At my studio, we surround ourselves with great photography. We are inspired by photographers like David Lachapelle, Yosuf Karsh, Patrick Demarchelier, Richard Avedon, and James Nachtwey, just to name a few. Renaissance painters are great to study as most of our lighting techniques come from them. They were the masters of turning a two-dimensional medium like a painting into a three-dimensional work of art. Great movies are another place to get wonderful ideas. Their compositions and lighting can be amazing. Personally, I was trained on lighting as a filmmaker and believe that it was a huge part of what makes me who I am today. Speaking of art, we can thank Greek and Roman sculptors for many of the poses we use today.

Inspiration is all around us. Whether it is in the future or in the past, we just need to tune into it. It is imperative to seek out work that you admire. I

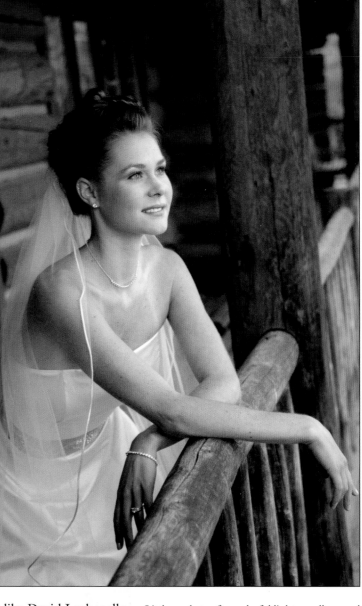

Little pockets of wonderful light are all around us. We just have to look for them. Here, overcast light from camera right illuminated the bride. The overhead light was blocked by the roof of the porch, creating soft shadows on her face. (**CAMERA:** Nikon D2X, **ISO:** 200, **LENS:** 50mm f/1.4, **EXPOSURE:** 1/250 second at f/2.8)

don't suggest you copy it, but let it inspire you. Emulate the qualities and characteristics you admire and make it your own. No one can afford to rest on their laurels. Ideally, we will all refine our skills constantly and strive to be better at every aspect of our profession.

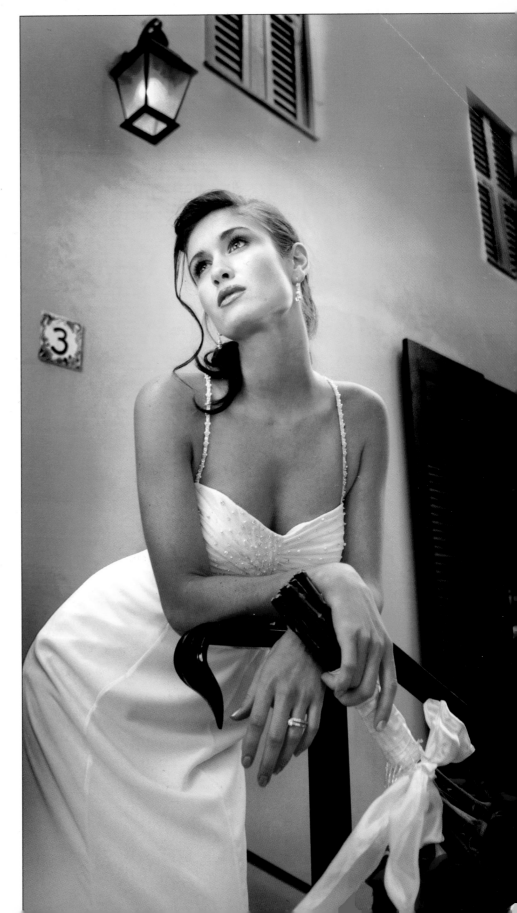

Today's bridal portraits are more fashion inspired than ever, so don't be afraid to use bold colors and untraditional poses—the results can be spectacular. (**CAMERA:** Nikon D2X, **ISO:** 100, **LENS:** 17–55mm at 18mm, **EXPOSURE:** $1/100$ second at f/2.8)

1. The Strategy

$\mathcal{W}$E HAVE A STRATEGY. THERE IS A METHOD TO OUR MADNESS. Our strategy employs a recipe for success under any circumstances. It has been used during hurricanes, tornadoes, rain storms and under sunny skies. Being a professional means consistently coming home with the goods—regardless of the circumstances.

BE PROACTIVE

Our photographers do not simply sit like flies on the wall and wait for things to unfold—we are very proactive. We are unobtrusive, but we are not afraid

The bride had laid out her wedding gown before we arrived, making a perfect getting-ready shot. This image is right out of the camera with no enhancement. (**CAMERA:** Nikon D1X, **ISO:** 800, **LENS:** 16mm, **EXPOSURE:** $^{1}/_{100}$ second at f/3.5, **LIGHTING:** available light, **OTHER:** tripod)

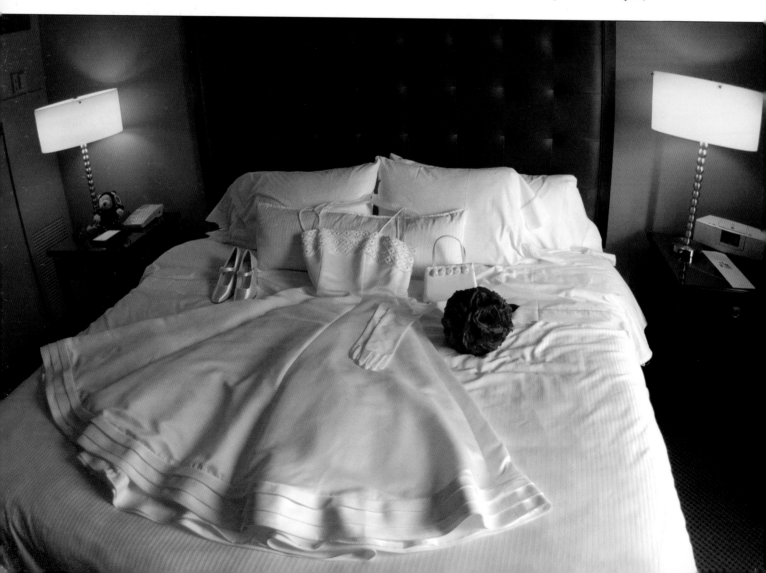

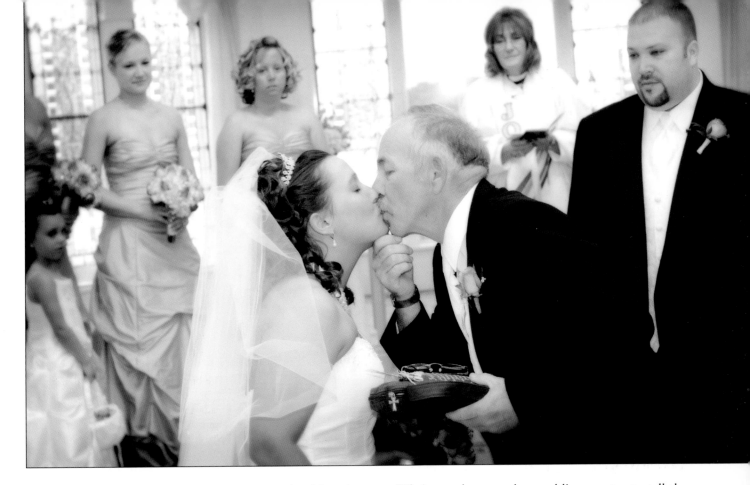

Some moments, like the father kissing his daughter, are easy to anticipate. (CAMERA: Nikon D2Xs, ISO: 640, LENS: 50mm f/1.4, EXPOSURE: $\frac{1}{60}$ second at f/5)

to make things happen. When we photograph a wedding, we try to tell the story of that event so that it can be recorded for posterity. Much like a writer or reporter, we cover the who, what, where, when, and why elements.

TAKE A NARRATIVE APPROACH

We approach our photo documentation like we are creating a photo essay. We take establishing shots everywhere we go: the bride's house, the ceremony site, the reception venue, and everywhere in between. We then look for details. Details, details, details. Visual attention to the details of a wedding will help propel your photography to the next level.

LEARN TO ANTICIPATE

We also zero in on the key players and look for the emotional moments that unfold during the day. You must train your perceptual vision to see everything around you. You must learn to anticipate what will happen. Some moments are expected, such as the father kissing the bride after walking her down the aisle, or a son kissing his mother at the end of the mother-son dance. It's important to consistently move around to find the best angle to cover these moments. Do not be rude or obtrusive, but do not be shy either. Get in, get your shot, and get out of the way.

GET THE EXPECTED SHOTS DONE EARLY

We are determined to tell the story of the day. Typically, we try to get all the expected shots out of the way in the first hour and a half—before the wedding has begun. This is when we capture the bride and groom with their parents (usually separately), as well the bride and groom with their attendants (also done separately). We believe these photos are important, but we shoot them quickly. We also do a quick bridal portrait at this time. Everyone is fresh and energized during these hours before the wedding, so it's a good time to capture these portraits while the sense of anticipation is still strong. We will get into this in more detail later in the book.

The foundation of our plan is to capture as many as possible of the portraits, family shots, and portfolio-type photos in the early hours of the day before the pace picks up. Once the ceremony rolls around, you won't have time to step away to experiment with different photographs. You'll also have less time to pull the wedding party and families away for posed pictures. So get the expected shots out of the way in the beginning. Then you can just have fun and let the day unfold.

After the ceremony—when people have shed their nervous energy and are more relaxed—is when you can capture those real moments that make every wedding day special. This will also be covered in greater detail later in the book.

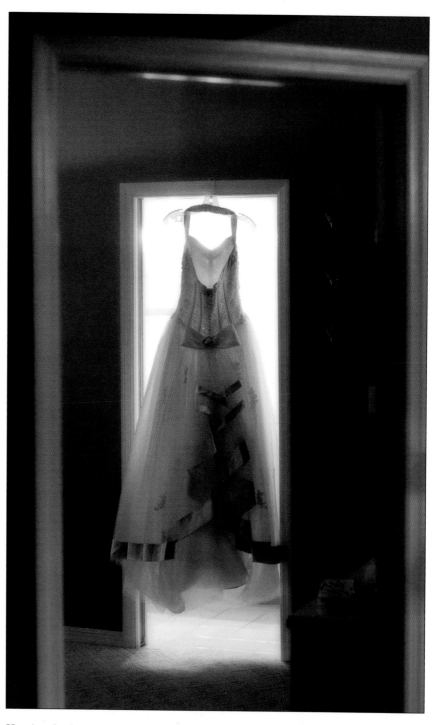

Hanging the dress in the doorway capitalized on the lighting. (CAMERA: Nikon D1X, ISO: 800, LENS: 50mm f/1.4, EXPOSURE: ¹⁄₆₀ second at f/2.8, LIGHTING: available light, OTHER: tripod)

2. The Consultation

A T MY STUDIO, WE FEEL THAT IT IS IMPORTANT for photographers to meet with the bride and groom personally. Our sales consultations are usually done either with the bride and groom, the bride and her mother, or just the bride.

IS IT A GOOD FIT?

The consultation is the best time to determine if this is the right client–artist fit. Today's brides are often quite savvy about photography and know buzzwords like "photojournalism" and "documentary style." However, all too often these terms mean something different to them than they do to us. It's important to communicate well and get on the same page. Although today's clients usually don't want hours of posed shots, it has been my experience that they do want a standard set of core photos. The key is to make sure that we are speaking the same language and that we are all working toward the same goals.

During the consultation, you can determine whether or not your style of photography is a good fit with the tastes of the bride and groom. (**CAMERA:** Nikon D2X, **ISO:** 320, **LENS:** 17–55mm at 30mm, **EXPOSURE:** ¹⁄₂₅₀ second at f/7.1)

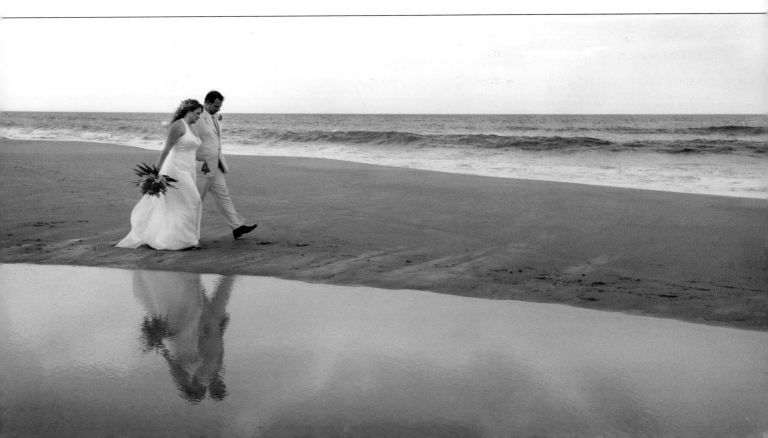

COVER THE BASICS

During the initial meeting with the client, we design a plan for a successful wedding day, outlining realistic expectations and a loose timeline. We ask questions about scheduling, when the ceremony starts, when the reception starts, and what sort of time we will have for photos in between events. We also find out if the couple is working with a coordinator or not, then establish the ceremony and reception locations. Coordinators can be a tremendous ally in making sure everyone is on time and in the right place. They can make your life very easy if you treat them with respect.

> FOR A TYPICAL WEDDING, WE START WITH THE BRIDE ABOUT NINETY MINUTES BEFORE THE WEDDING.

OUR APPROACH

Next, we outline our loose approach to the day. For a typical wedding, we start with the bride about ninety minutes before the wedding. She will either be getting ready at the church, in a hotel, or at home. We will ask if it is possible for her bridesmaids to be completely dressed and ready when we arrive. We also request that the bride's hair and makeup be completed, but that she is not yet in her dress at this time. We like to get a shot of the gown hanging up or lying on a bed, because it sets the tone for the beginning of the

The bridesmaids' bouquets make an excellent "getting ready" shot. (CAMERA: Nikon D2Xs, ISO: 400, LENS: 17–55mm at 35mm, EXPOSURE: 1/25 second at f/2.8, LIGHTING: available light, OTHER: tripod)

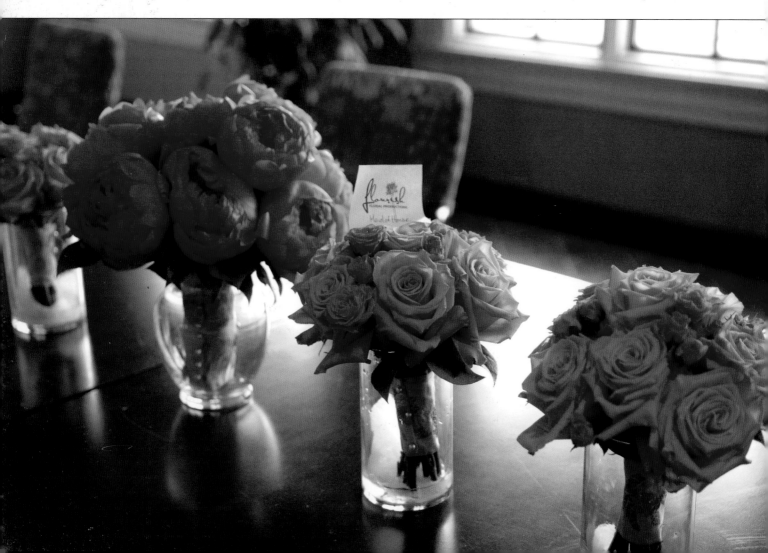

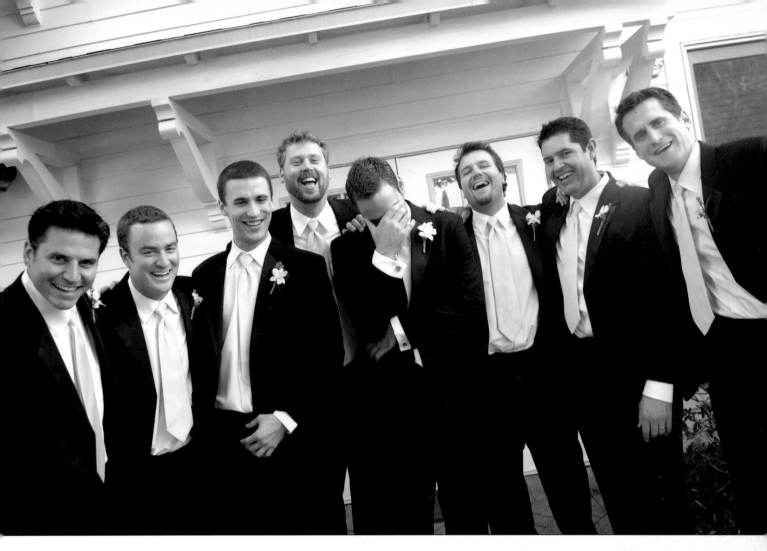

When the guys are getting ready, the moments in between the shots can be priceless. (**CAMERA:** Nikon D2X, **ISO:** 100, **LENS:** 17–55mm f/2.8 at 17mm, **EXPOSURE:** $^1/_{125}$ second at f/2.8)

story of the day. I always work with an assistant or associate photographer, preferably a female, who will have an advantage in capturing the bride while she is putting on her dress.

During the first several minutes that our photographers are onsite, we will usually shoot details such as the dress, shoes, and flowers. This only takes about fifteen minutes. Next, the bride will hopefully be ready to put on her dress. A female associate goes in to capture the initial shots and signals when the bride is fully dressed. We then continue with the "getting ready" shots (which are detailed in chapter 4).

The next step is to take all the bridesmaids, the bride, and her parents downstairs or outside—usually to an open-shade area with a nondescript background. In about fifteen minutes, we photograph each bridesmaid individually with the bride, then grab a group shot. We will also photograph the parents separately and then together with the bride. After that, we spend about twenty minutes on the bride alone. We are careful not to stray too far, but you will be amazed what you can get while everything is fresh and pretty before the ceremony.

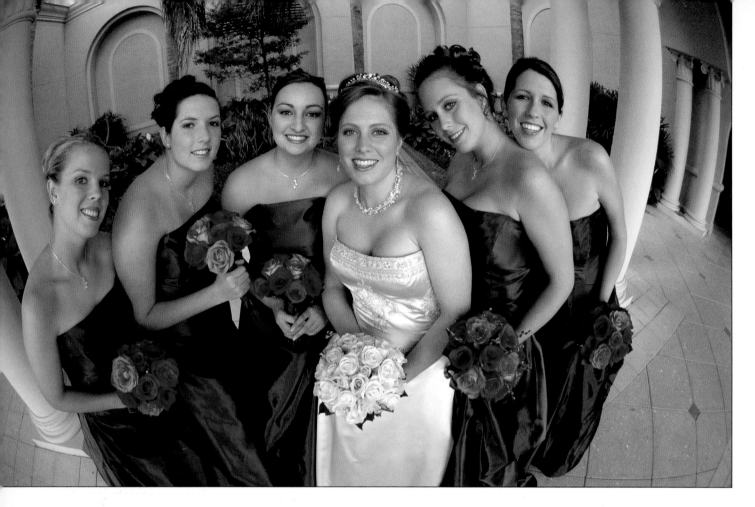

The entire process with the bride's party takes around forty-five minutes to an hour to complete. Ideally, you want to have her safely hidden away about thirty minutes prior to the wedding. Otherwise, the mother of the bride, minister, and coordinator get a little nervous about the bride being seen too early.

Nobody seems to mind if the groom is walking around in plain view prior to the ceremony, though, so we photograph him after the bride. Grooms typically only require about fifteen minutes to photograph. We photograph the groom with each groomsman, followed by a group shot. As with the bride, we then photograph the groom's parents separately, and then capture some images of just the groom.

Once these principal shots are out of the way, we get ready for the ceremony. Because we work a two-photographer system, we try to get different perspectives if circumstances and the location permit.

After the ceremony, the next time crunch involves getting the family shots. I suggest capturing all of the main players first. We will typically pose the bride and groom, then add the bride's parents followed by her immediate family and grandparents. Next up are the groom's parents, and the same routine follows.

Photographing the bride and bridesmaids before the ceremony helps get some of the expected pictures out of the way. (**CAMERA:** Nikon D70s, **ISO:** 200, **LENS:** 10.5mm fish-eye, **EXPOSURE:** 1/125 second at f/3.5)

Following the family shots, we pose the bridal party and then aim to spend about twenty-five to thirty-five minutes with the bride and groom. Any other group shots (aunts, uncles, school or work friends) that time doesn't allow for can be made up at the reception. This gives us more time with the bride and groom.

After the money shots of the bride and groom (see chapter 7), we head for the reception site and document the room before the couple and guests arrive. Once the guests enter and the happy couple is announced, we simply do our best to document the party.

LATER, AT THE RECEPTION, THE DRINKS WILL BE FLOWING AND PEOPLE WILL LOOSEN UP . . .

Using this system, over the course of an eight-hour wedding the bride may only have to pose for about eighty minutes or so, and the groom will be involved in the picture-taking for about only about forty-five minutes. The rest of the time is theirs to have fun. In addition to letting the bride and groom spend more time celebrating with their guests, this approach also lets you hedge your bets—you get all of the expected shots out of the way in the beginning, making sure to get the more traditional family shots that will please the parents and grandparents. Doing it in those early hours also lets you shoot the posed images while people are more reserved and not yet interested in letting their hair down. Later, at the reception, the drinks will be

If the circumstances permit, a wide view like this makes a wonderful establishing shot. (**CAMERA:** Nikon D2Xs, **ISO:** 800, **LENS:** 17–55mm at 30mm, **EXPOSURE:** 1/60 second at f/2.8, **OTHER:** tripod)

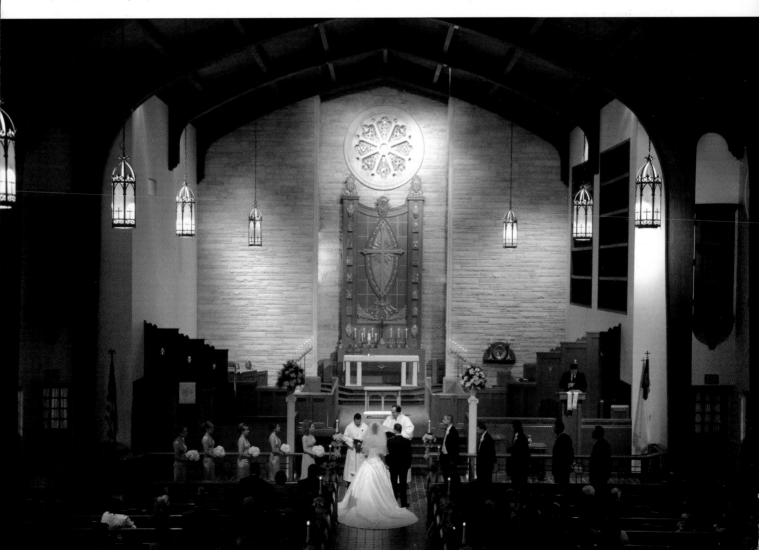

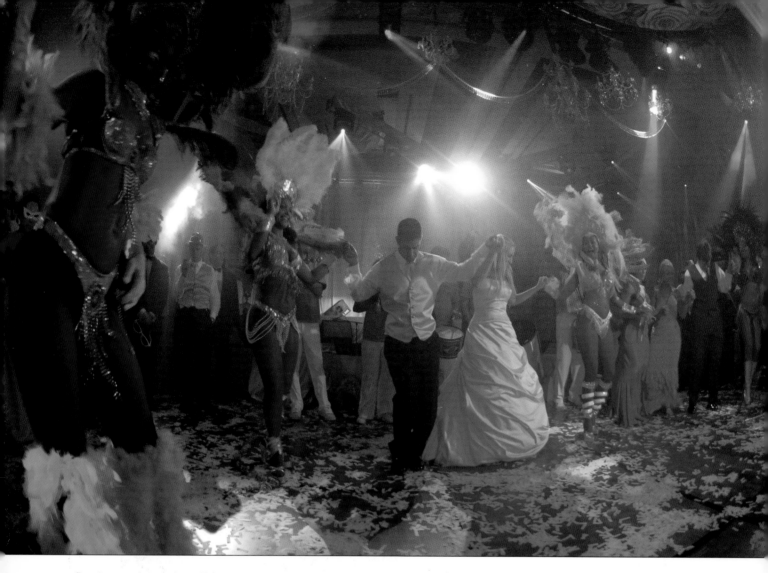

flowing and people will loosen up—and that's when you can look for more "real" moments to capture.

During the initial consultation, we explain that this is our preferred approach—but if everything goes to hell in a hand basket, we will just document the event journalistically. For example, at one wedding I worked, a tornado destroyed the reception site just an hour before the guests were scheduled to arrive! The show had to go on, though. Luckily, the bride went with the flow and we all ended up having a lot of fun. You can never predict events like this, so it's a good idea to make your clients aware that, sometimes, everything doesn't go exactly as planned.

As the reception kicks into high gear, look for shots of people cutting loose. Here, the bride and groom dance with colorful carnivale performers. (**CAMERA:** Nikon D200, **ISO:** 800, **LENS:** 10.5mm fisheye, **EXPOSURE:** $\frac{1}{40}$ second at f/2.8)

3. Gathering the Gear

$\mathcal{A}$ PLACE FOR EVERYTHING AND EVERYTHING IN ITS PLACE. This adage sounds like a no-brainer, but many photographers' gear is a mess. During the wedding day, there are a lot of things you can't control. Your gear, however, is not one of those things.

Keeping your gear organized means a little less chaos to deal with on a busy wedding shoot.

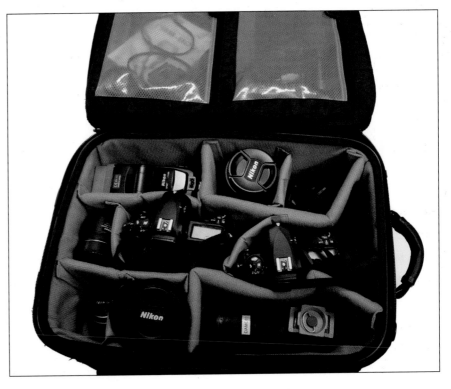

PACK IT YOURSELF

I feel that it is important for a photographer to pack for his or her own shoot. If you let your assistant pack and something is forgotten, it can create tension throughout the shoot. Just take the time to do it yourself and you'll be happier. Create a checklist and have your assistant confirm everything before you leave. The key is to double and triple check that you have everything you need. When you see the perfect shot for your fisheye lens and then discover it is not in your bag, you will be sorry. These moments are fleeting so you need to be prepared. Even if you get a last-minute call and have to run out the door for the job, having everything organized in advance will make these emergency situations much easier to handle.

DON'T WAIT UNTIL THE LAST MINUTE

Prep your equipment the night or day before. Make sure all of your batteries are charged and you have enough cleaned memory cards (all images deleted and the cards formatted) for the upcoming event. Clean your lenses with a micro-fiber cloth and air spray. Check that your camera sensors are spotless, as well.

OUR KIT

A rolling case, such as the Lowepro Pro Roller 1, is an excellent asset. It is generous enough to fit about two full systems and will qualify as an airline carry on. We have memorized where everything goes and use two of these rolling cases, one for cameras and one for lights. I also keep two light stands, two tripods and two umbrellas or reflectors with me at all times.

You need a minimum of one camera body for your main shooter. Ideally, the main photographer should have one camera body and the associate photographer should have one (we take two Nikon D3 digital SLRs). If one body should malfunction, the main shooter can then use the associate's camera as an emergency backup. This is the system we employ. We also have standby gear that an off-duty associate can bring to us in a pinch. This is a good arrangement if you have a support system, such as nearby family members or other studio employees. Photographers who choose to work alone should always have a main and backup body. The bottom line is that you need to be prepared for anything.

AS A PROFESSIONAL, YOU NEED TO COME HOME WITH THE GOODS EVERY TIME. THERE ARE NO EXCUSES.

We also pack a range of Nikkor lenses: a 16mm f/2.8 fisheye; a 50mm f/1.4; an AF micro 60mm f/2.8; an 85mm f/1.4; a 17–35mm f/2.8; a 24–70mm f/2.8; and an 80–200mm f/2.8. However, I recommend that novice wedding photographers keep it simple. Concentrate on a couple lenses that you know how to use well, and then work your way up to a more complete arsenal.

BACKUP, BACKUP, BACKUP

One of the mantras for this book is that, as a professional, you need to come home with the goods every time. There are no excuses and few opportunities to reshoot after an event. So always, *always* have backup equipment—

Stay lean and mean by securing surplus gear and carrying only what you need.

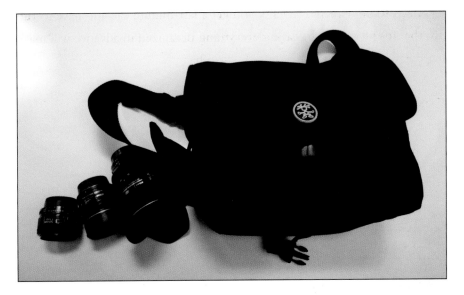

even if your reserve camera is a lesser-quality unit. I can't stress this enough: backup, backup your backup, and backup the backup to your backup.

. . . But Don't Overload Yourself

While it's important to have adequate backup equipment, don't overload yourself while you're out shooting. Having too much gear can distract you from what is going on right in front of you. We prefer to stay lean and mean, so we take in only what we need for each part of the wedding. We want to be observers capturing moments, not fiddling with lenses while the moment comes and goes. I like to use one camera at a time. Some photographers like to carry two camera bodies with different lenses, but I find that shooting with two can be cumbersome, and the cameras tend to bump into each other. Plus, it can be a real drag on your neck. In our system, the associate holds the shoulder bag and tripod while the main shooter creates great images. (*Note:* Of course, the two-camera system does have some advantages as well; it's all just personal preference.)

Secure Your Gear

We always make sure our spare equipment is safely locked in our vehicle or in a secure room at the event site. For example, when we go in to capture the bride getting ready, we usually bring a tripod, reflector, and Nikon D3. In a small, over-the-shoulder camera bag, we also pack four lenses: a 17–35mm f/2.8; a 24–70mm f/2.8; a 16mm f/2.8 fisheye; and an 80–200mm f/2.8. Everything else stays locked up.

4. Getting Ready

WE LIKE TO GET MOST OF THE EXPECTED SHOTS out of the way in the first hour. We usually start an hour and a half before the ceremony and capture the getting-ready shots at the beginning of our shooting. We will start wherever the bride is dressing for the wedding. Our first capture is often an establishing shot of the scene, and then we move inside to work with the bridal party.

WHAT TO SHOOT

We usually have one camera body, a tripod, a fisheye lens, three zoom lenses (17–35mm, 24–70mm, and 80–200mm), and a flash. If the clients have listened to our suggestions from the consultation, the dress will be displayed and everyone will be ready for pictures. We will document the dress, shoes, and anything special in the room. We are also on the lookout for special notes, cards, or presents from the groom. A lot of times, these gifts will be delivered while you are in the room, and it's great to add them to the other detail shots.

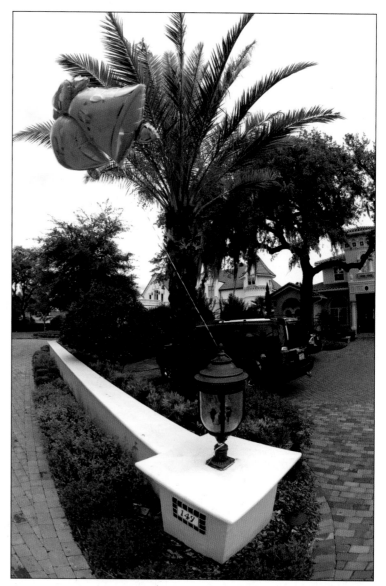

Right—An image of the exterior of the bride's home makes a good establishing shot for the "getting ready" phase of the wedding. (**CAMERA:** Nikon D2Xs, **ISO:** 160, **LENS:** 10.5mm fisheye, **EXPOSURE:** $\frac{1}{320}$ second at f/5.6)

Facing Page—A photograph of the dress laid out for the bride is perfect for beginning the story of the day. (**CAMERA:** Nikon D2Xs, **ISO:** 800, **LENS:** 10.5mm fisheye, **EXPOSURE:** $\frac{1}{100}$ second at f/2.8, **LIGHTING:** available light)

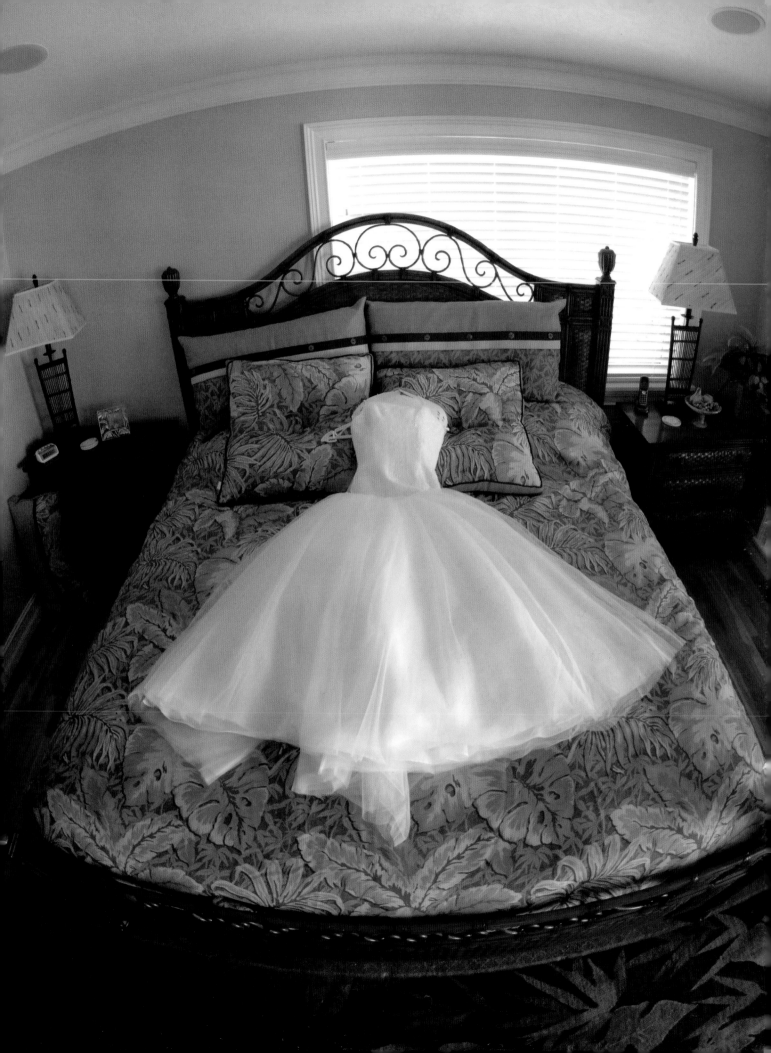

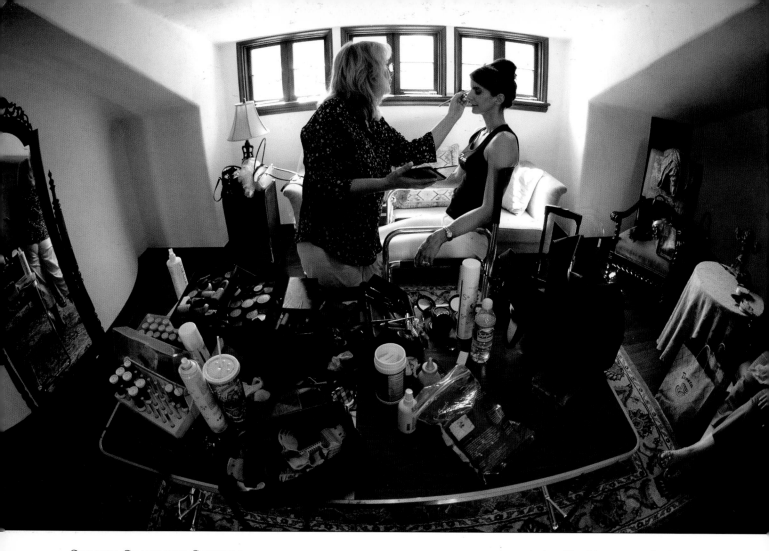

SET THE STAGE FOR SUCCESS

Wedding photography is not just about photography. You need to know how to act appropriately. It is almost part show, part photography. During the pre-ceremony time, you will be spending a lot of time with the bridal party, and your interaction can affect the tone of the day. To set the right mood, we are very patient. We have a wish list of certain shots we would like to achieve, but we do not like to rush people.

It is best to be low key at this point in the wedding day. We like a "fly on the wall" approach that allows us to tune in to the climate of the day. If you watch and listen carefully, you will quickly determine the main players—and you might pick up on any touchy hot buttons of the day. It always helps to know if there are family members who don't get along, certain people who don't want to be photographed together, or particular guests who must be given special attention. Also, our studio believes in calling people by their first names. During these early moments of the day, we memorize the names of the members of the bridal party as well as those of the close family members who are present.

A shot like this captures the feeling of the very involved process a bride goes through as she gets ready for the wedding. (CAMERA: Nikon D1X, ISO: 800, LENS: 10.5mm fish-eye, EXPOSURE: 1/50 second at f/2.8, LIGHT-ING: available light, OTHER: tripod)

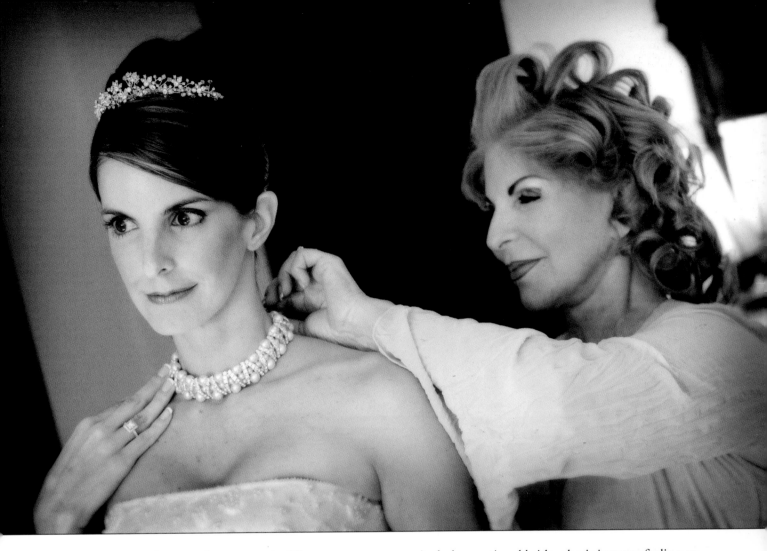

Try to capture emotional moments between the key players as the bride is getting ready. (CAMERA: Nikon D2X, ISO: 800, LENS: 17–55mm at 48mm, EXPOSURE: 1/80 second at f/2.8)

If you encounter a particularly emotional bride who is just not feeling co-operative, go with the flow. Try to tactfully and gently keep her on track, but don't force things. Do your best to work around her. Get images of the bridesmaids and the details. Give her some time to pull it together. When it is necessary to involve her in the photographs, mention that it would be a good time to get the dress on or that it would be great to get a few shots of her with the bridesmaids before the ceremony. If she declines, it was her decision. Do your best to make it up later in the day, but also tactfully make those involved aware that they are partnering with you to get great photographs. If they are unwilling to participate, make sure you've given them the option—just in case they get angry later on that you didn't capture certain images. You want to accommodate your clients as much as possible, but you can't force things. Just remember: this is their special day, not yours. (*Note:* When things get challenging, it's also a great time to employ a more journalistic style of coverage, ensuring appropriate documentation of the important people, places, and things.)

THE BRIDE GETTING DRESSED

Once you have familiarized yourself with everyone and caught up on the juicy gossip, it is time for the bride to get dressed. Our studio usually has a female associate who photographs the bride at this time. The associate tries to get tasteful yet sexy shots of the dressing process. Female photographers have an advantage during these moments, because their presence is less awkward for the bride—she may even try to pose for a shot or two.

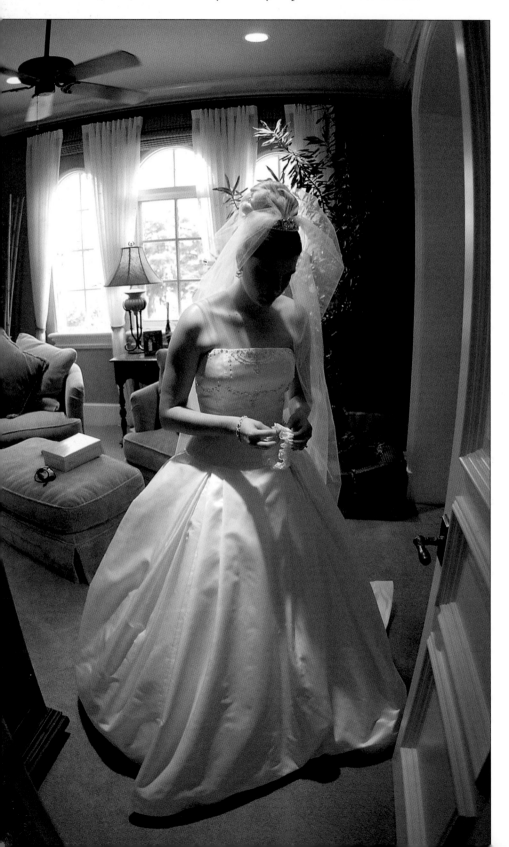

These silent moments can be very powerful. It's almost like watching an athlete meditating before the big game. (CAMERA: Nikon D1X, ISO: 800, LENS: 16mm f/2.8, EXPOSURE: $\frac{1}{160}$ second at f/2.8)

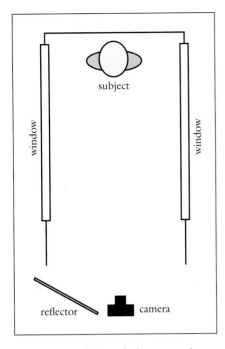

This portrait, which took about two minutes to create, was shot right outside the room where the bride was getting ready. (**CAMERA:** Nikon D2Xs, **ISO:** 500, **LENS:** 50mm f/1.4, **EXPOSURE:** ¹⁄₁₂₅ second at f/2.8, **LIGHTING:** available light)

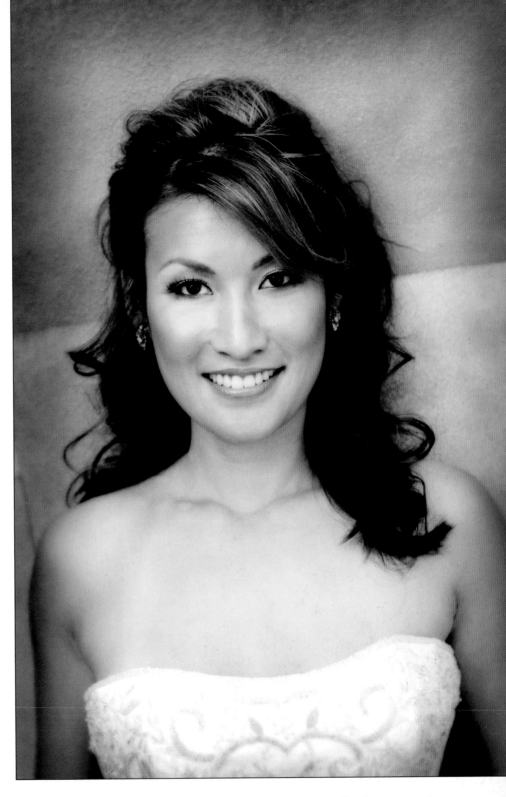

Once the bride is mostly dressed, I enter and resume the documentation process as the main photographer. This is typically when the mom or maid of honor is buttoning or lacing up the back of the bride's dress. This is also a good time to photograph the mom or maid of honor helping the bride put on her shoes, garter, jewelry, and other accessories. Look for real emotions, especially between mother and daughter.

The next thing we like to do is capture a couple shots of the bride. First, we do an available light headshot. Next, we shoot a full-length portrait from the back and perhaps a mirror shot. Capturing these images now, inside in a climate-controlled room, ensures that the bride, her dress, her hair, and her flowers will be as fresh as they are going to be. This session is an excellent opportunity to capture a few portfolio pieces.

Posed Images of the Bride, Bridesmaids, and Family

After the session with the bride, we take the bride, bridesmaids, and the bride's parents down to an open shade location with a neutral background.

Facing Page, Top—The bride and bridesmaids were posed for this image before the ceremony, getting one of the expected posed shots out of the way. (CAMERA: Nikon D2X, ISO: 250, LENS: 10.5mm fisheye, EXPOSURE: $\frac{1}{125}$ second at f/4.5)

Facing Page, Bottom Left—This shot was made using the existing canned lighting in the ceiling as the main light. (CAMERA: Nikon D2X, ISO: 800, LENS: 17–55mm f/2.8 at 17mm, EXPOSURE: $\frac{1}{13}$ second at f/2.8, OTHER: tripod)

Facing Page, Bottom Right—A shot like this is a good way to show off the back of the dress and incorporate the surroundings. (CAMERA: Nikon D2X, ISO: 800, LENS: 17–55mm f/2.8 at 22mm, EXPOSURE: $\frac{1}{160}$ second at f/2.8)

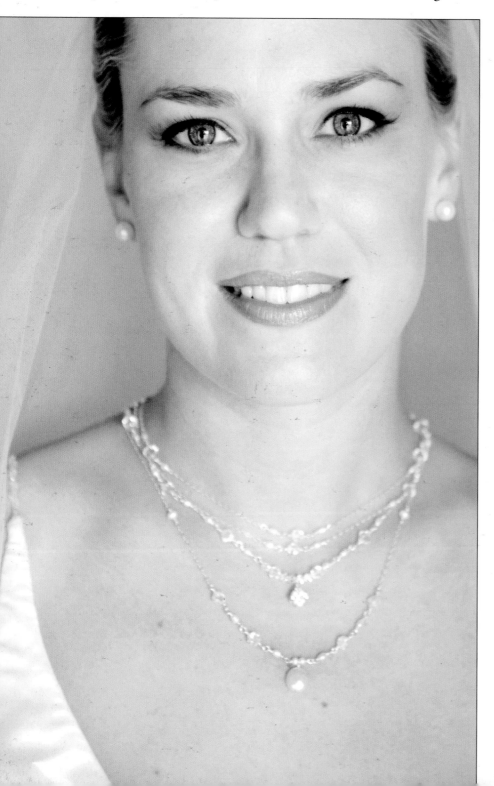

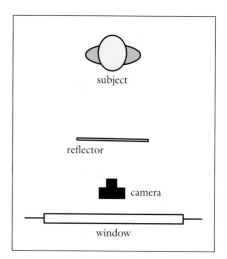

Here, the bride was photographed by window light in the room where she was getting dressed. (CAMERA: Nikon D2Xs, ISO: 500, LENS: 50mm f/1.4, EXPOSURE: $\frac{1}{60}$ second at f/2.8)

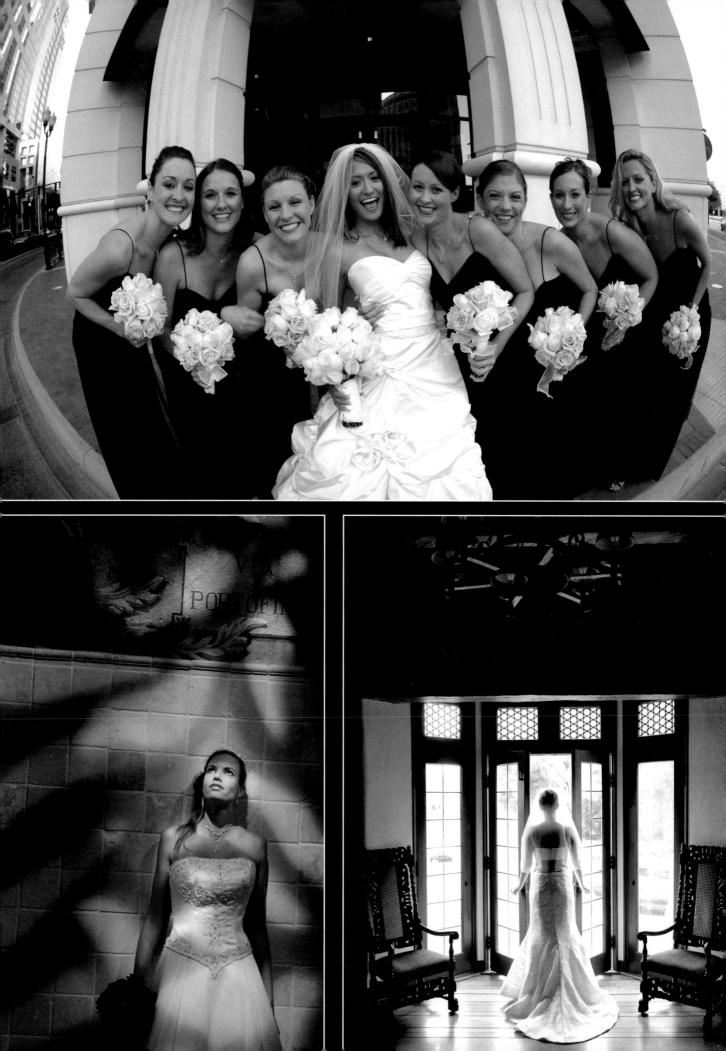

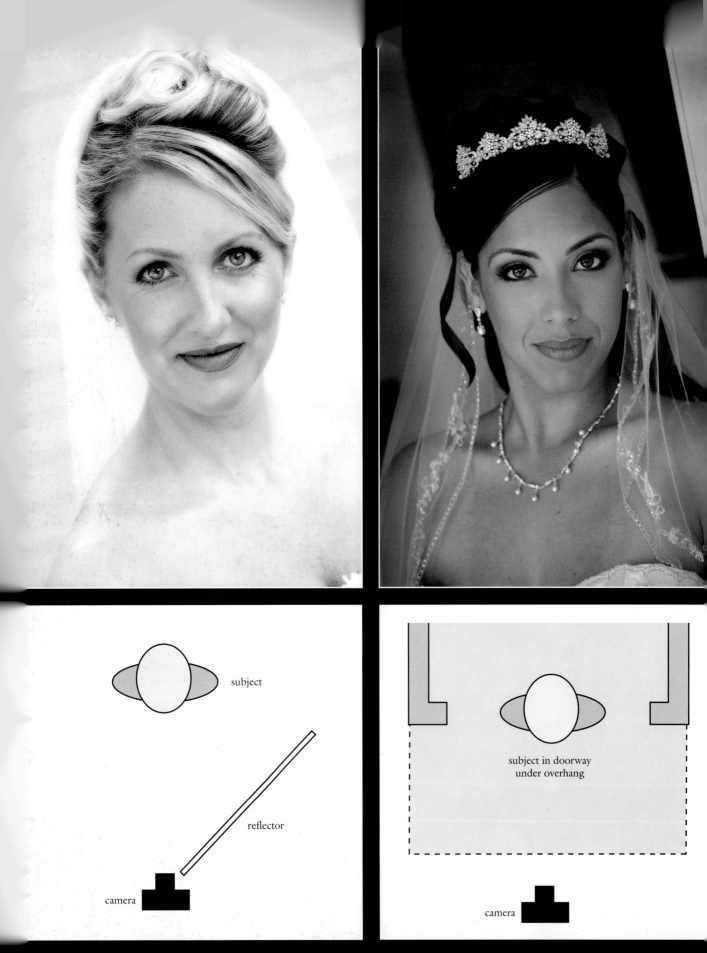

subject

reflector

camera

subject in doorway
under overhang

camera

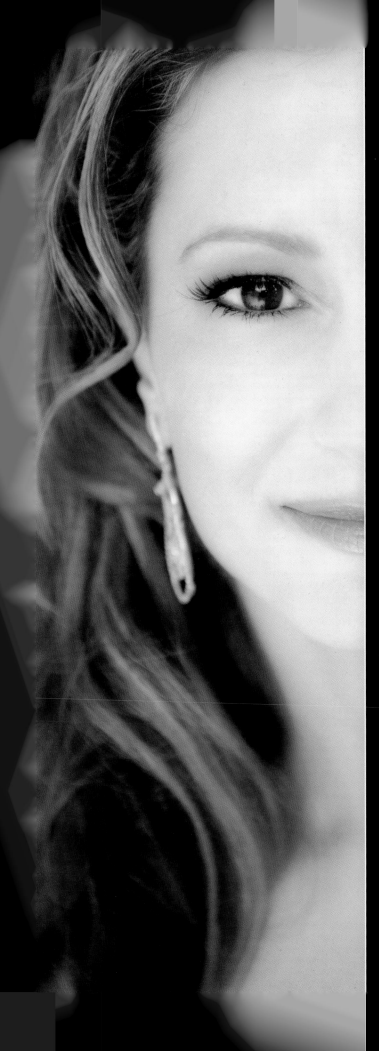

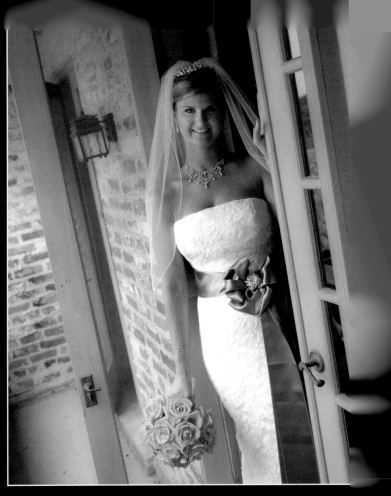

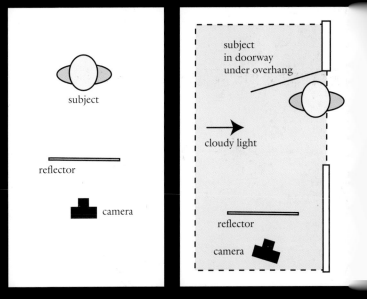

Left and Left Diagram—The unusual cropping of this bridal portrait vio lates the viewer's expectations, making for a more dramatic image. (CAM ERA: Nikon D2X, ISO: 100, LENS: 17–55mm f/2.8 at 55mm, EXPOSURE ¹⁄₁₂₅ second at f/2.8)

Above and Right Diagram—When shooting a bridal portrait, look for col ors and textures to add interest to each shot. (CAMERA: Nikon D2X, ISO 400, LENS: 17–55mm at 22mm, EXPOSURE: ¹⁄₁₆₀ second at f/2.8)

We have coordinated this with the groom so he won't be walking around and run into us. We quickly photograph each bridesmaid with the bride. Then we shoot a group shot of the bridesmaids and the bride. Finally, we photograph the mom with the bride, dad with the bride, and then all three together.

Next, we'll spend fifteen to twenty minutes doing a mini photo shoot with the bride alone. We try to incorporate the flavor of the wedding location into a contemporary portrait of the bride. We don't get too crazy at this time, because we do not want the bride to get sweaty or flustered. We are also

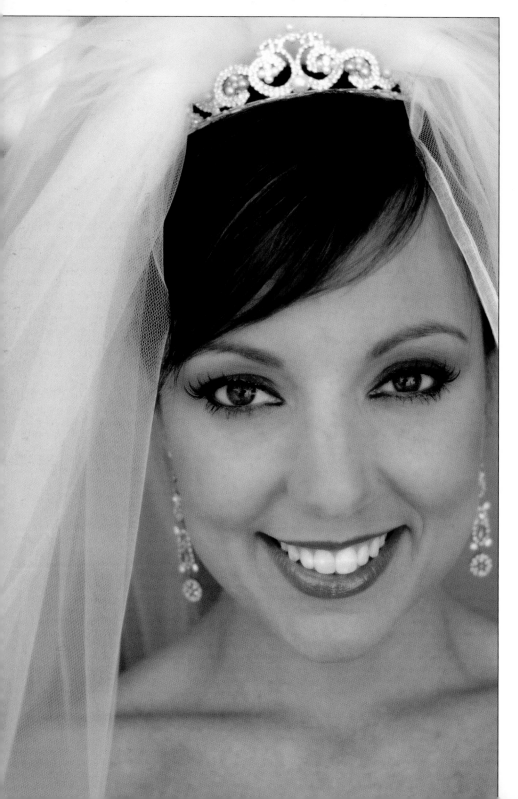

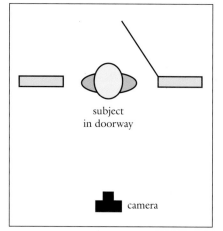

When the bride was done getting ready, this lovely portrait was shot in the doorway of her home. (CAMERA: Nikon D2Xs, ISO: 160, LENS: 50mm f/1.4, EXPOSURE: $\frac{1}{160}$ second at f/4)

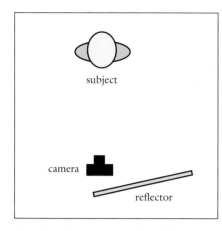

subject

camera

reflector

Shooting this bridal portrait at f/2.8 helped throw the very distracting background out of focus. (**CAMERA:** Nikon D2X, **ISO:** 200, **LENS:** 80–200mm at 92mm, **EXPOSURE:** $\frac{1}{400}$ second at f/2.8)

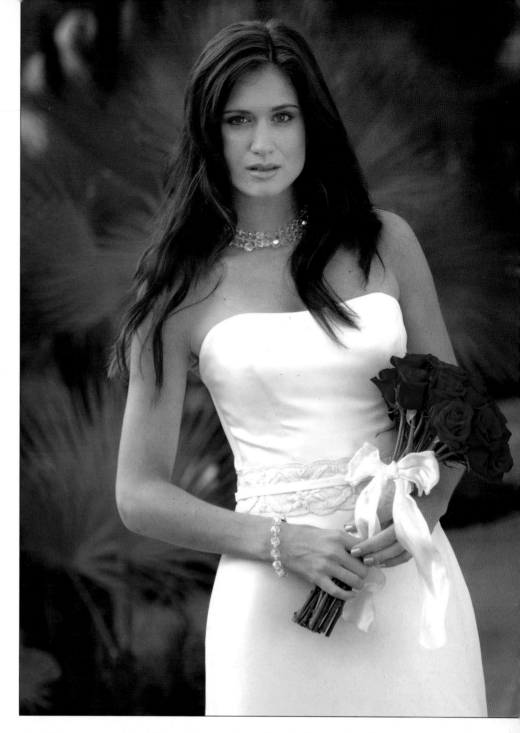

mindful not to get her dress dirty and usually ask the maid of honor to help with the train. We also carry a sheet to lay down under the dress. If you don't have a sheet you can usually score some towels, tablecloths, or sheets from the venue—especially if you are at a hotel or the bride's home.

All of the pre-ceremony photography takes about an hour. About thirty minutes before the ceremony you should have the bride back in her holding room. Even in these modern times, mothers, priests, coordinators, and guests get bent out of shape if people see the bride before the wedding. We go with the flow and respect their wishes.

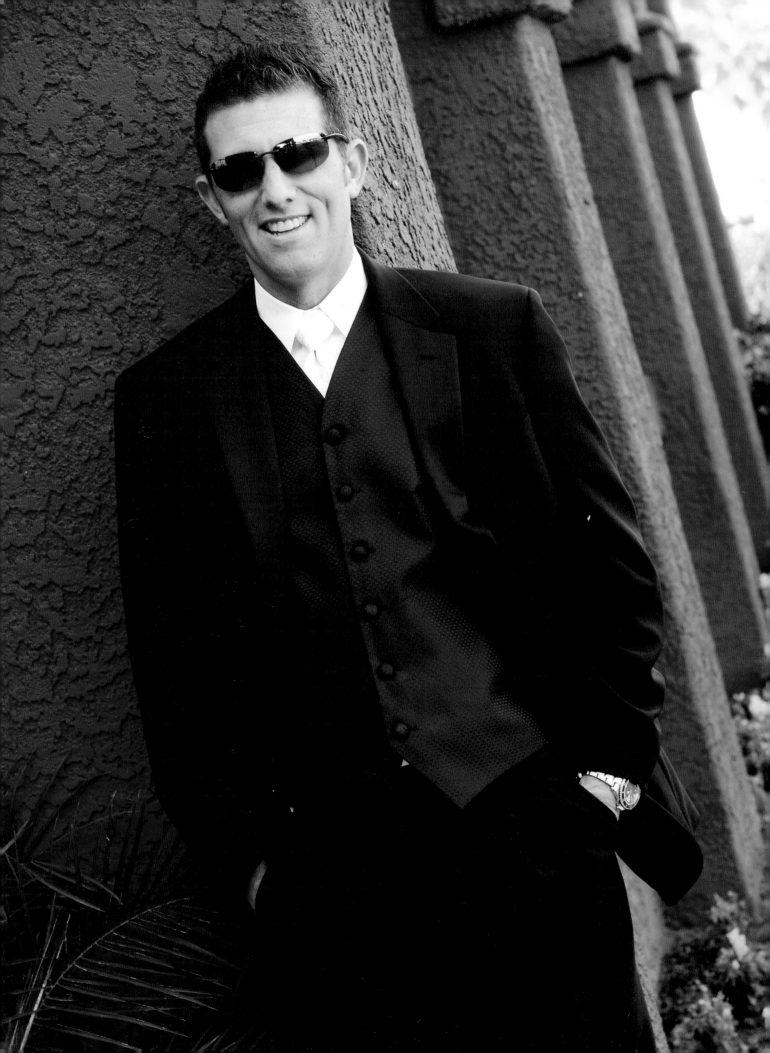

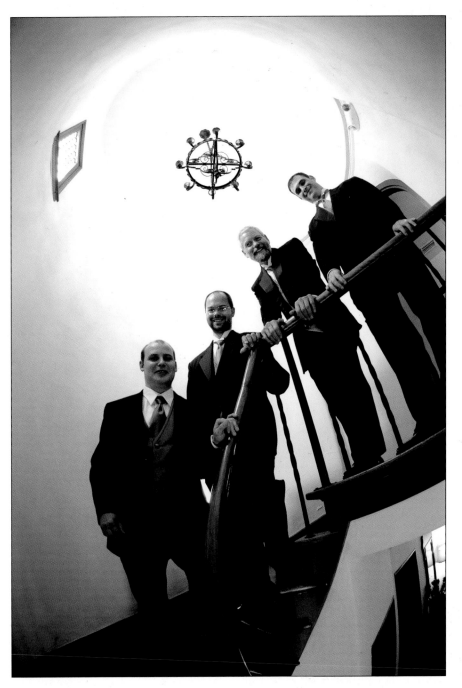

In a few instances (usually evening ceremonies where a lack of available light after the event will prohibit shooting) the bride and groom may opt to see each other before the event. This is great for the photographer as you can get almost all the posed shots out of the way in the beginning. In this case, we usually stage a special meeting where the bride and groom see each other for the first time in their wedding attire. There are two of us shooting simultaneously and we capture the individual as well as overall emotional reactions. In the days of film, photographers often pushed for this. Nowadays, we let the bride and groom decide—and we only suggest this option when it is in their best interests in terms of the lighting. In our experience this happens less than ten percent of the time.

PORTRAITS OF THE GUYS

Now it's time for the guys! We typically meet the guys at the ceremony site thirty minutes prior to the wedding. We do not usually photograph them getting dressed; that only happens at a celebrity or high-profile

Facing Page—With male subjects, having them lean against the wall puts the subject at ease and creates a more relaxed look. (CAMERA: Nikon D2Xs, ISO: 320, LENS: 50mm f/1.4, EXPOSURE: ¹⁄₁₀₀ second at f/5)

Above—Using a fisheye lens makes for a dynamic group shot that incorporates the venue. (CAMERA: Nikon D70s, ISO: 800, LENS: 10.5mm fisheye, EXPOSURE: ¹⁄₂₅ second at f/2.8)

wedding when we use a team of four photographers. Normally we will shoot each groomsman with the groom and then grab a shot of all the groomsmen together with the groom. Be mindful that you must photograph the ushers first, because they will need to start performing their duties as soon as guests begin arriving. When we're done with the groomsmen, we photograph the groom with his mother, the groom with his father, and then all three together. Next, we will shoot a few pictures of the groom on his own. All of these photos take place in about fifteen minutes.

5. The Ceremony

THE CEREMONY IS THE CULMINATION of months of planning for the happy couple. It is a sacred experience. Brides and grooms are often in a trance-like state during their wedding ceremonies, and the whole event can go by for them in a blur. Your photos, capturing each special moment, will be an everlasting reminder of what really happened—all the little details they may have missed in the flurry of activities and emotions.

RESPECT THE VENUE'S RULES

It is important for the photographer to know how to act appropriately. Some venues are stricter than others. For example, at many outdoor venues you have carte-blanche freedom to roam around. Inside churches or temples, however, you are usually more restricted. Even when given total freedom, be respectful of the event. Do not linger in front of the parents or the guests. Get in, get your shot, and get out. Even though this may be your tenth, hundredth, or thousandth ceremony, chances are it's a first for the bride and groom, so try to be as unobtrusive as possible.

In a church or temple wedding, you must first meet and befriend the ceremony site's li-

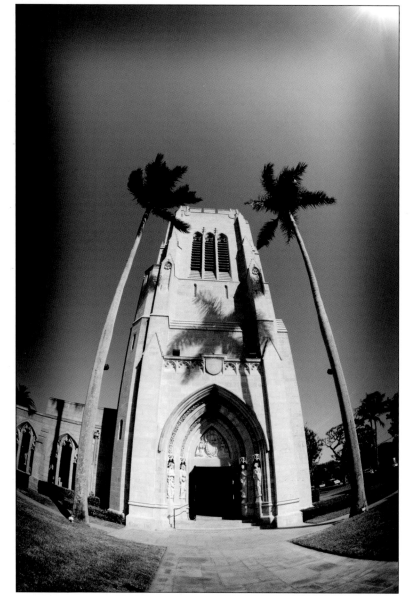

A dramatic establishing shot of Bethesda by the Sea in Palm Beach, FL. (CAMERA: Nikon D2Xs, ISO: 100, LENS: 10.5mm fisheye, EXPOSURE: ¹/₂₅₀ second at f/10)

This image captures a ceremony detail and an establishing shot in one frame. (**CAMERA:** Nikon D1X, **ISO:** 400, **LENS:** 16mm, **EXPOSURE:** ¹⁄₂₀₀ second at f/3.5)

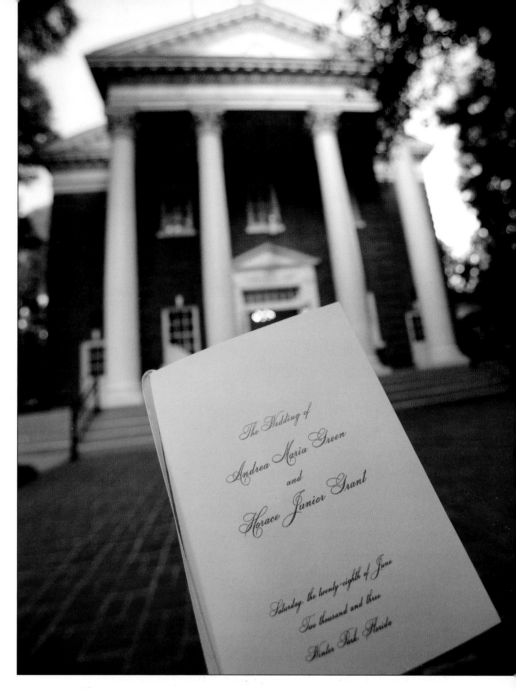

aison. Most churches and temples have specific rules about what a photographer is allowed to do. If you introduce yourself and acknowledge these rules, you will usually put them at ease. If you do not, they will have a watchful eye on you and they can make your life difficult. Keep in mind that these officials are just doing their job and trying to preserve the sanctity of the experience. If you develop a good relationship, they will remember you and often give you more leeway the next time you shoot there. Conversely, if you ignore their rules, your next shoot will be a living hell. Some venues have even blackballed vendors for inappropriate acts, and it is not uncommon for the celebrant to stop in the middle of the ceremony and verbally chastise the out-of-bounds photographer. (*Note:* After the wedding, it never hurts to follow up with the ceremony-site liaison and offer some prints or a CD of images of their venue. That will buy you preferential treatment the next time you photograph there.)

All places of worship differ slightly in their strictness and rules. Many venues post their rules on their Web sites. Typically, the rules are as follows:

- Photographers are allowed to use flash during the processional and recessional only.
- Photographers may shoot from the back third or behind the last row of seated guests from the middle aisle.
- Photographers are expected to shoot the processional and then move out of the aisle into the pew.

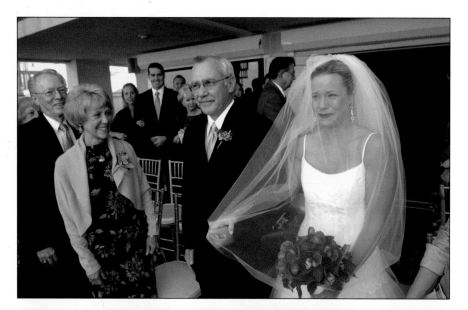

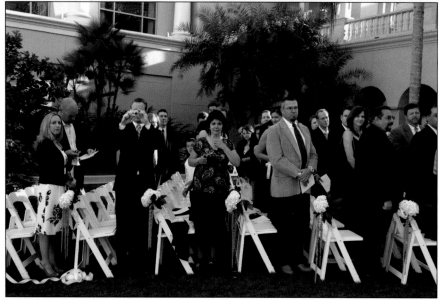

Top—The entrance of the bride and her father is an important image to capture—and especially memorable when it's as emotional as this one. (**CAMERA:** Nikon D2Xs, **ISO:** 400, **LENS:** 17–55mm at 17mm, **EXPOSURE:** $\frac{1}{250}$ second at f/4)

Bottom—Don't forget to record the reactions of the guests as the members of the bridal party appear. (**CAMERA:** Nikon D2Xs, **ISO:** 400, **LENS:** 17–55mm at 26mm, **EXPOSURE:** $\frac{1}{125}$ second at f/5.6)

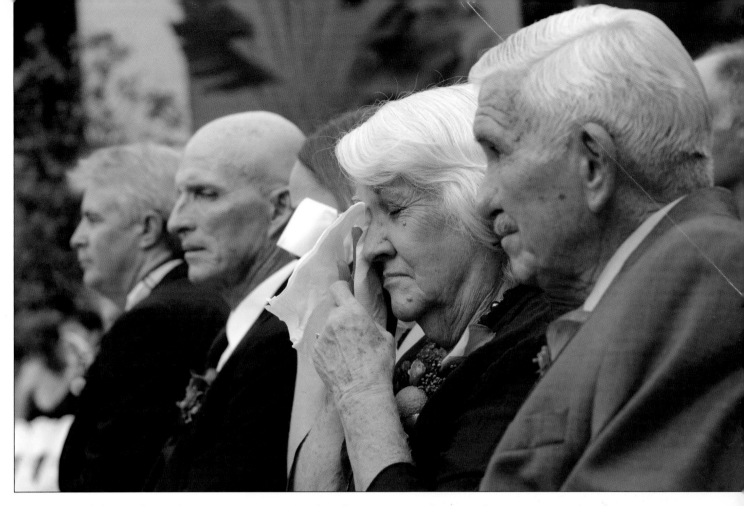

Having a second shooter during the ceremony makes it easier to capture the emotions of the guests. (**CAMERA:** Nikon D2X, **ISO:** 400, **LENS:** 70–200mm at 70mm, **EXPOSURE:** 1/400 second at f/5)

- During the ceremony, photographers are expected to stay behind the last row of guests and are not allowed to use any flash photography.
- Photographers can expect to share space and work courteously with the videographer.
- Sites with balconies sometimes restrict the photographers to shooting only from the balcony.

These are the most common rules at ceremony sites, but you never know what you will encounter. There is a church in central Florida where they shut the doors and you must photograph the ceremony through a porthole in the door! The videographer, however, is allowed inside. Go figure.

When we shoot an event at a church, we ask ahead of time if one of our photographers can set up to the side of the altar with a tripod. Churches don't like a lot of movement, so it puts them at ease if you tell them you will be stationary and working on a tripod. If they permit this, we can capture nice shots of the reactions of the bride, groom, parents, and wedding party during the ceremony. The photographer at the back of the church will then do most of the documentation of the event itself.

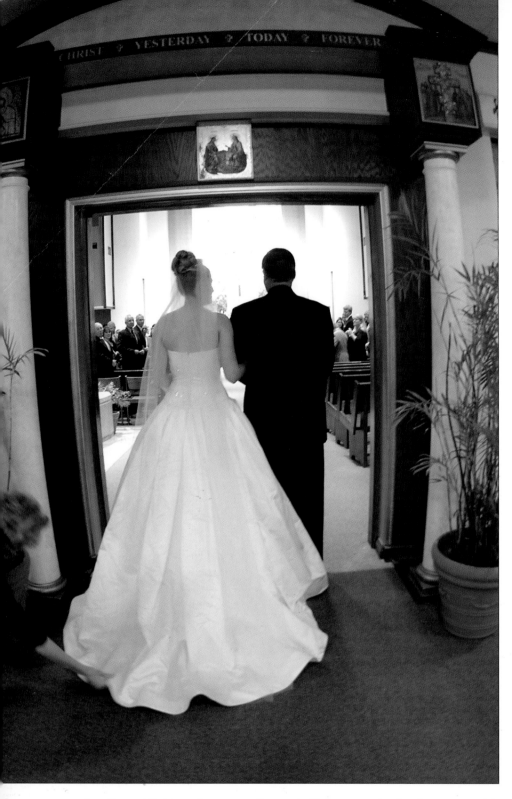

Here, our second shooter was able to capture a rear view of the bride and her father just about to walk down the aisle. (**CAMERA:** Nikon D100, **ISO:** 800, **LENS:** 16mm fisheye, **EXPOSURE:** $^1\!/_{200}$ second at f/5)

Another trick is to plant one of your staff as a guest in the front row with the parents. To pull this off, you definitely need the parents and clients to be on board. The planted photographer will only be able to shoot a few poignant moments before putting the camera away. If they are snapping away throughout the ceremony, the celebrant will tell them to knock it off. Save this trick for huge events and be courteous if you employ it.

Two Photographers

Typically, our studio has two photographers covering the ceremony. One will capture the processional and images from inside the sanctuary. The other will hang with the bride during those nervous last moments. They will also try to capture the bride's entrance from the back as she walks down the aisle. Once the ceremony begins, both photographers stay in one place with their tripods. As noted above, ideally this entails having one photographer to the side of the altar and another at the back of the church.

Exposure

We often shoot ceremonies with 80–200mm lenses. We set our ISO to 800 and shoot with exposures anywhere from f/2.8 at $\frac{1}{100}$ second to f/2.8 at $\frac{1}{20}$ second. Most of the churches and temples we encounter have lighting that lets us work as f/2.8 at $\frac{1}{60}$ second at 800 ISO. (*Note:* The new Nikon D3 allows us to shoot at ISOs up to 6400. The 1600 setting provides really nice results; 3200 and 6400 are noisier. Still, we usually try to shoot at as low an ISO as we can. This is generally still around 800, but it's nice to know that the D3 can effectively shoot at higher settings and still provide a professional-quality image.)

When you have a second shooter, he or she can work on getting some unusual angles, such as this shot of the bride over the groom's shoulder. (CAMERA: Nikon D2X, ISO: 100, LENS: 70-200mm at 98mm, EXPOSURE: $\frac{1}{200}$ second at f/5)

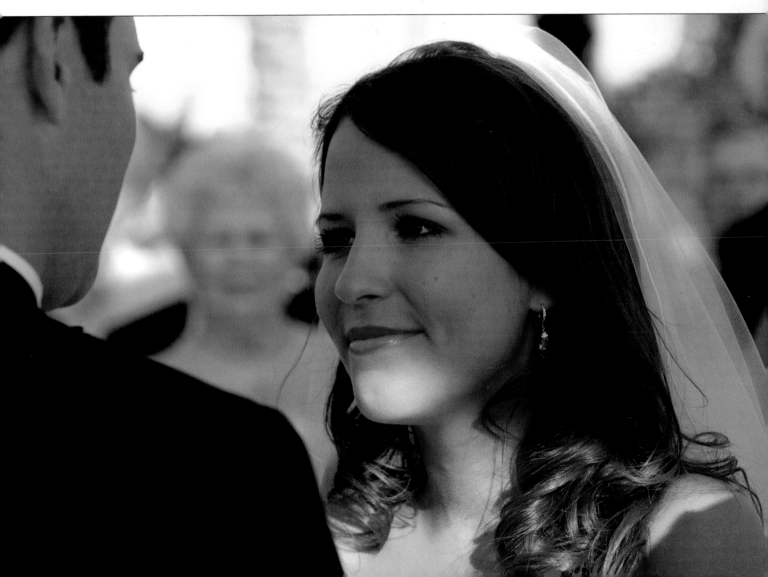

Even though we are prohibited from using flash during the ceremony, we do not mind because on-camera flash tends to wash out and flatten the ambience of the available light. We prefer to shoot wide open and select the fastest shutter speed we can get away with. The depth of field is not really an issue, but focus is critical; you must zero in exactly on your subject. If you must shoot as low as ½0 second, be advised that only about one in five shots will be useable. Of course, shooting from a tripod will help to ensure sharp focus. You can also achieve an above-average

ON-CAMERA FLASH TENDS TO WASH OUT AND FLATTEN THE AMBIENCE OF THE AVAILABLE LIGHT.

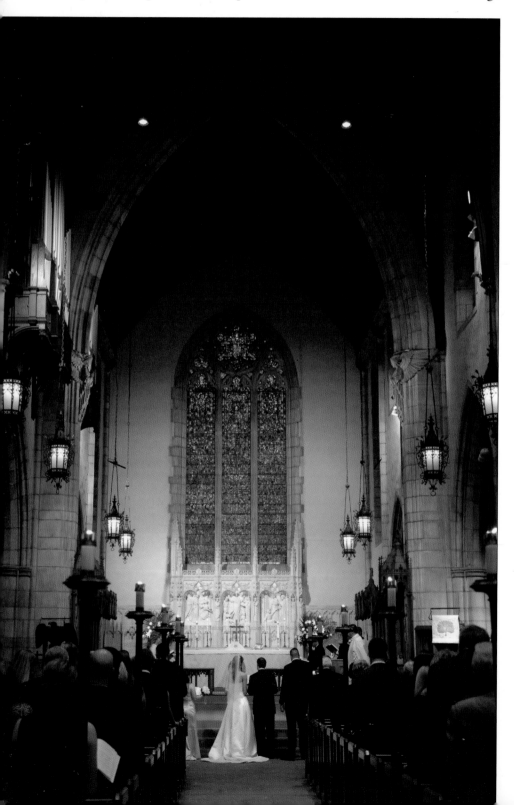

This grand image was shot from the back of the church and would make a great establishing shot in the couple's album. (CAMERA: Nikon D2Xs, ISO: 800, LENS: 17–55mm at 34mm, EXPOSURE: ¹⁄₄₀ second at f/2.8, OTHER: tripod)

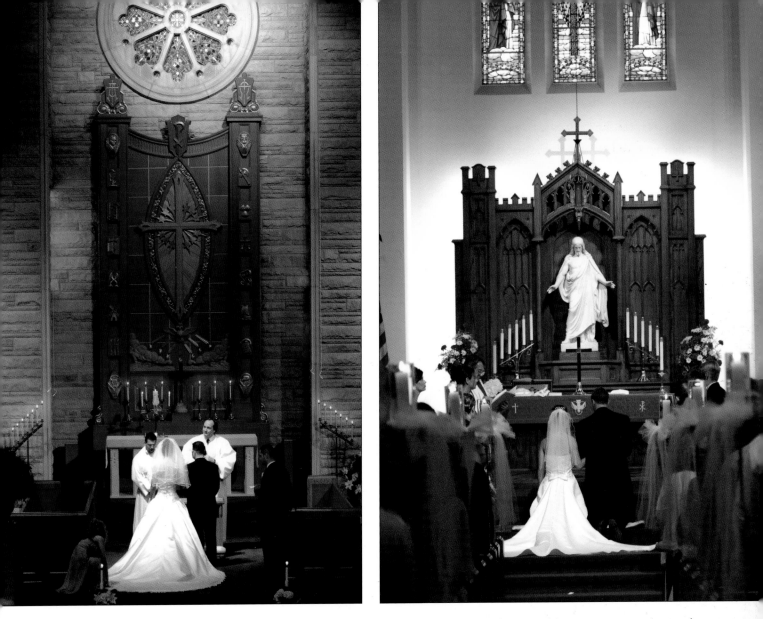

Left—Shooting with available light only is the best way to capture the depth and beauty of the scene. (CAMERA: Nikon D2Xs, ISO: 800, LENS: 80–200mm, EXPOSURE: ¹⁄₈₀ second at f/2.8, OTHER: tripod)

Right—If the venue allows it, moving forward down the center aisle allows you to capture a tighter shot of the bride and groom at the altar. (CAMERA: Nikon D1X, ISO: 800, LENS: 80–200mm at 80mm, EXPOSURE: ¹⁄₁₀₀ second at f/2.8, OTHER: tripod)

number of useable images by waiting until your subjects are not moving and then doing a burst of about three exposures. (*Note:* For exposure tips when shooting outdoor weddings, see pages 52–53).

WHITE BALANCE

Our photographers ascertain the white balance for the church when they arrive. Usually, we use the automatic or tungsten white balance setting. Sometimes, however, we create a custom white balance setting with an ExpoDisc. The ExpoDisc is great in mixed lighting conditions and could not be easier to use with the Nikon cameras. We use the 77mm neutral ExpoDisc, which is large enough to fit all of our lenses. To use it, you simply set your camera to the custom white balance setting (on Nikons, the symbol for this is PRE). Then, hold the WB button until it blinks. Next, make your exposure while holding the disc over the lens. We usually focus, then turn the auto focus off and make the exposure. It will either say "Good" or "NG" for not good. If it says NG, we just drag the shutter or overexpose it a little to get a proper reading. That's it—your white balance is set for that area. If you turn to a differently lit part of the site, then it may require another custom white balancing.

Sometimes we shoot scenes on all three settings (automatic, tungsten, and custom) and decide what we like best when we see images on the computer. With the advent of Adobe Lightroom and RAW files, it's a snap to make mass color corrections in postproduction.

Now that we have our white balance, we document the event like any other story. We start with some wide-angle establishing shots, then some medium shots, and then telephoto images.

WATCH FOR KEY MOMENTS

Most church ceremonies last from twenty minutes to one hour. The average time is probably thirty-five minutes. This is ample time to get all the shots you need. This is one time during the wedding day when you are not rushed, so take your time and try to immerse yourself in the ceremony. Be cognizant of your subjects. Vigilantly look for expressions.

At the beginning of the ceremony, the first thing the shooter at the front of the church should look out for is when the celebrant asks, "Who gives this woman to this man?" or something similar. The father will reply, "Her mother and I do." Then he will usually give her a kiss on the cheek. Be ready.

The shooter at the rear of the church is responsible for the overall shots, but they also have the best angle on some parts of the ceremony. The ring

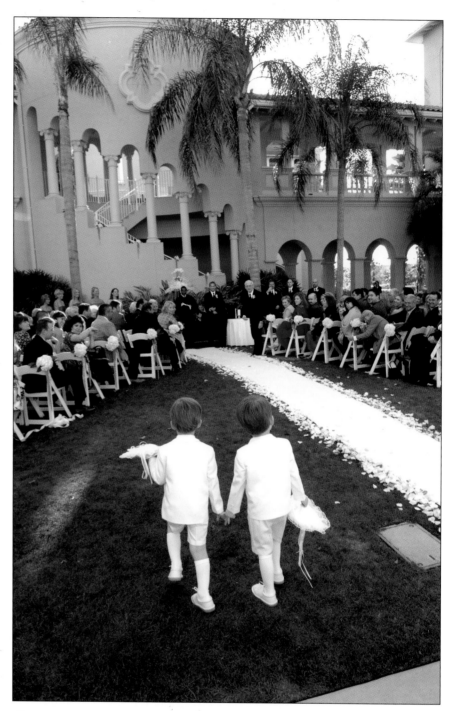

Above—Using a wide angle lens made it possible to capture both the adorable ring bearers and the guests' reactions. (CAMERA: Nikon D2Xs, ISO: 400, LENS: 17–55mm at 17mm, EXPOSURE: $\frac{1}{160}$ second at f/5.6)

Facing Page—Flower girl shots are always popular, and they make great establishing shots. (CAMERA: Nikon D2X, ISO: 100, LENS: 10.5mm fisheye, EXPOSURE: $\frac{1}{250}$ second at f/9)

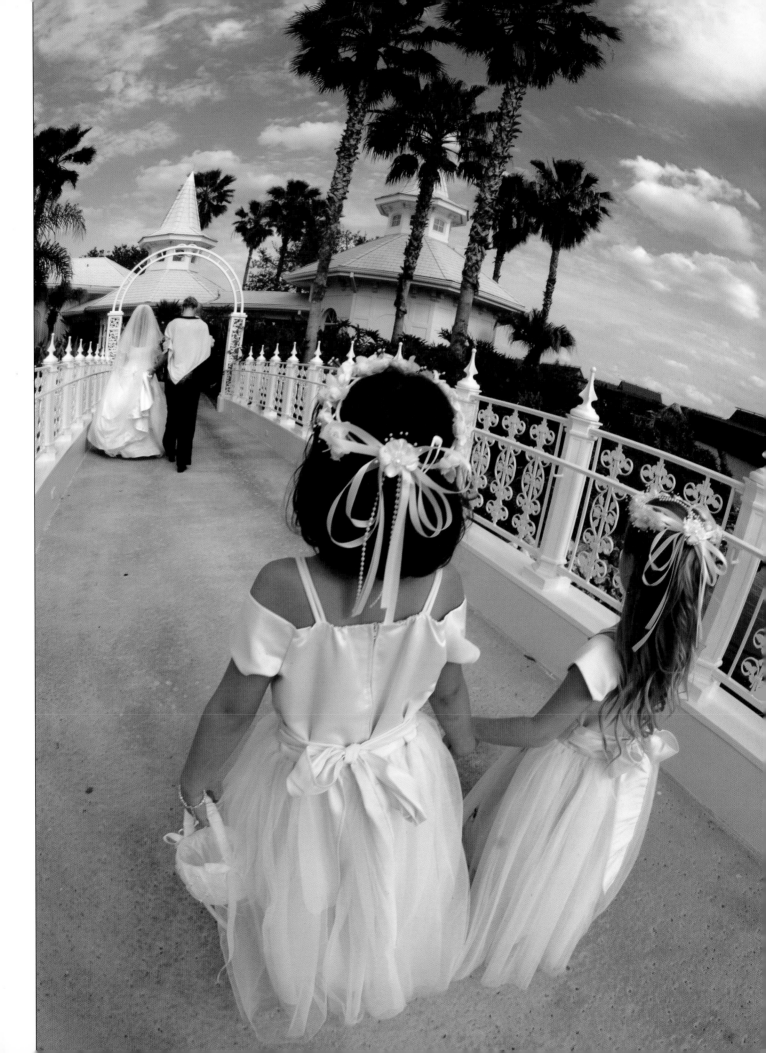

exchange, communion, lighting of the unity candle, and the first kiss are usually best photographed from this position, so anticipate and be ready for these events.

UNDERSTAND THE TRADITIONS

Most of the ceremony specifics we've discussed so far revolve around traditional Christian weddings. However, it's important not to ignore other religious traditions—particularly Jewish and Hindu ceremonies. These are huge markets and it would behoove any wedding photographer who wants to make a living to embrace them.

It has been our experience that the young people in these cultures yearn for a more contemporary style of photography. Because of this, they often look beyond the traditional vendors of their culture. Many couples would rather have a more modern style and teach you their traditions than be stuck with someone who knows their traditions intimately but whose style of documenting it may not be as contemporary. The savvy photographer will proactively learn these traditions and position themselves for success.

Hindu ceremonies are very beautiful, spectacular events. The colors are vibrant, and it is a pleasant departure to photograph something other than white dresses and black tuxedos. The people are gracious and festive, and the

IT IS A PLEASANT DEPARTURE TO PHOTOGRAPH SOMETHING OTHER THAN WHITE DRESSES AND BLACK TUXEDOS.

Eight hundred people attended this Indian wedding. (**CAMERA:** Nikon D1X, **ISO:** 200, **LENS:** 10.5mm fisheye, **EXPOSURE:** 1/100 second at f/5.0)

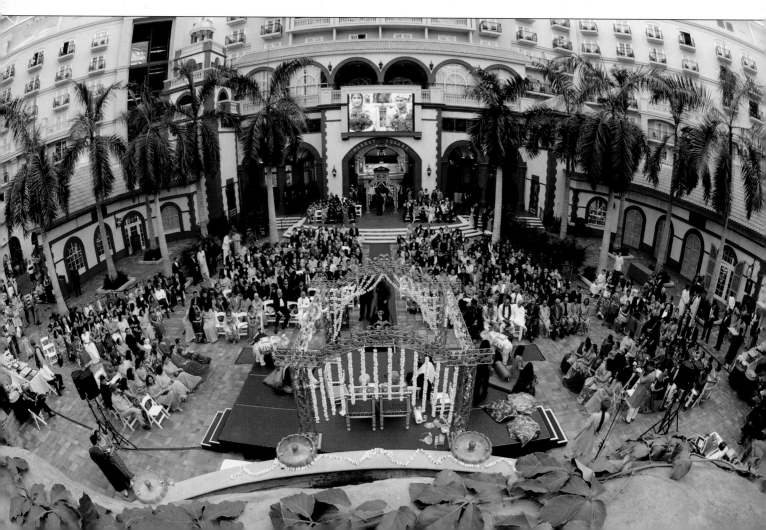

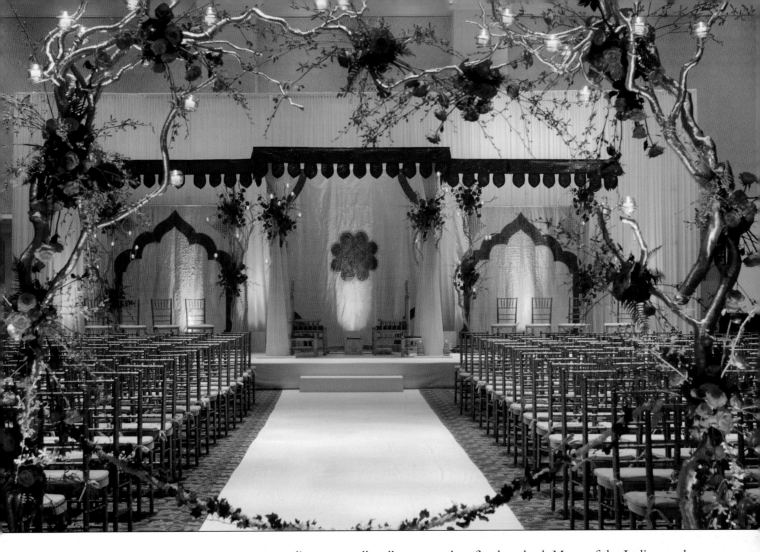

The setup for a Hindu wedding. (CAMERA: Nikon D1X, ISO: 400, LENS: 17–55mm at 48mm, EXPOSURE: ¼ second at f/5.6, OTHER: tripod)

guest lists can swell well to more than five hundred. Many of the Indian weddings we have covered have involved three different events: the garba, the Mendhi, and the actual wedding ceremony. Be advised that these events may span several days. They are very rewarding photographically, but they are a lot of work. So, when asked to provide a quote for an Indian wedding, bid accordingly.

If you are unfamiliar with Hindu wedding traditions, do some research before tackling such an event. The client will help you learn some of their traditions during the planning process, but you need to do your homework as well. During the ceremony, the couple will often assign a family member to help guide the photographer. These liaisons are a valuable asset and you should take advantage of their insight to make sure you don't miss anything.

During many Hindu ceremonies, there are few (if any) restrictions placed on the photographer. You generally have full access to position yourself and move around. At some points during the event you may even need to be a little aggressive. For example, pho-

DURING MANY HINDU CEREMONIES, THERE ARE FEW (IF ANY) RESTRICTIONS PLACED ON THE PHOTOGRAPHER.

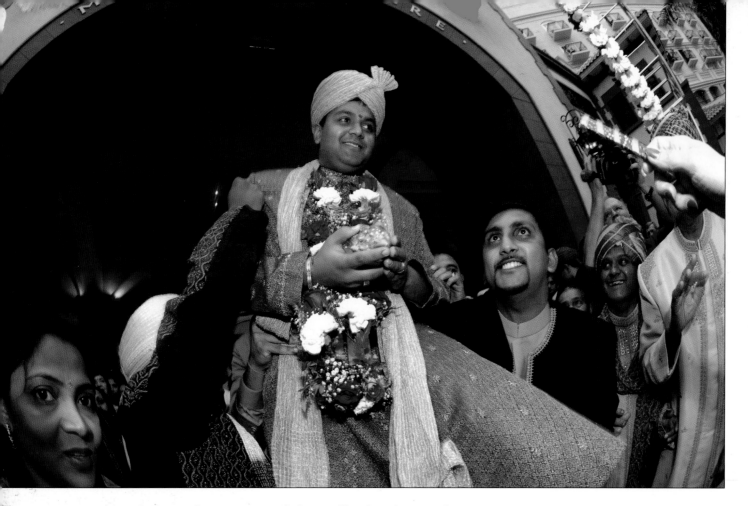

tographing the groom's entrance can feel more like shooting a rock concert from the mosh pit than photographing a religious ceremony!

Jewish weddings are also rich with wonderful traditions and require some education to document properly. At Walt Disney World, the Rabbi who performed services at the Pavilion taught me (and the other non-Jewish photographers) the key elements of the Jewish ceremony. While there is much information online pertaining to Jewish weddings, it is my experience that one-on-one counseling is the way to go. If you approach your local synagogue, you might be surprised that the Rabbi will be more than happy to educate you about the fine points of the Jewish wedding ritual.

One important challenge for photographers is that the ceremony is not traditionally held until after sundown. This makes for some long exposures at outdoor events.

OUTDOOR CEREMONIES

Now let's discuss another ceremony type that we frequently have in Central Florida: the outdoor ceremony. Some advantages to the outdoor ceremony are free access to position yourself and ample lighting. Some drawbacks are that they are often only fifteen minutes long and the weather can provide

Above—The groom is accompanied to the venue by his relatives and friends, who arrive dancing and rejoicing. (CAMERA: Nikon D2X, ISO: 100, LENS: 10.5mm fisheye, EXPOSURE: 1/60 second at f/5.6, OTHER: on-camera flash)

Facing Page, Top—Jewish weddings are traditionally held after sunset, making for long exposures when shooting outdoors. (CAMERA: Nikon D2X, ISO: 800, LENS: 10.5mm fisheye, EXPOSURE: 1/2 second at f/5.6, OTHER: tripod)

Facing Page, Bottom—The chuppah, a four-poled canopy, is an important element of most Jewish wedding ceremonies. (CAMERA: Nikon D2X, ISO: 100, LENS: 10.5mm fisheye, EXPOSURE: 1/60 second at f/5.6, OTHER: tripod)

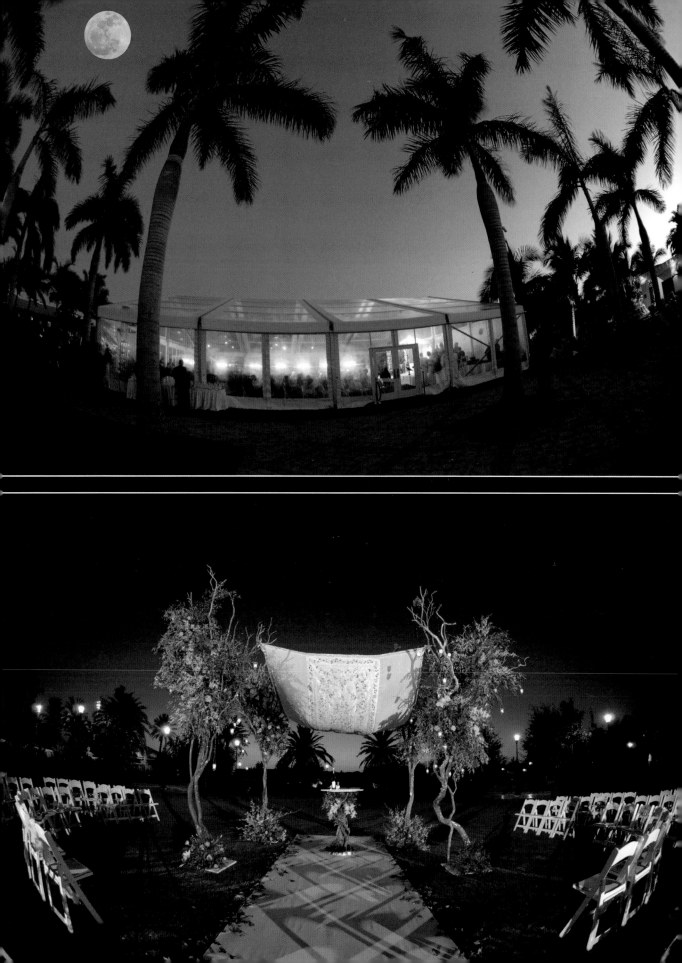

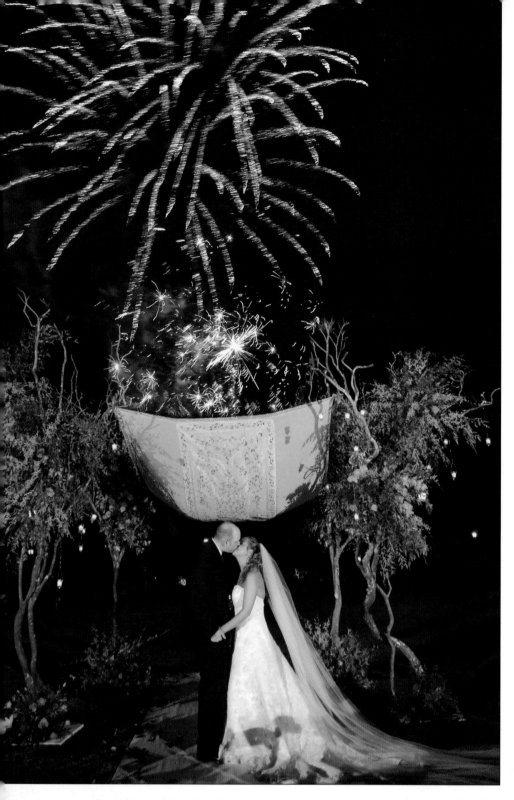

some problems. Usually, though, outdoor events can be quite splendid. You just have to work fast.

As with an indoor ceremony, we coordinate our two photographers to capture the entire event from multiple angles. One photographer sets up in the middle aisle and one works from the back. The major difference is that you do not need to be on a tripod as there is ample light to handhold your

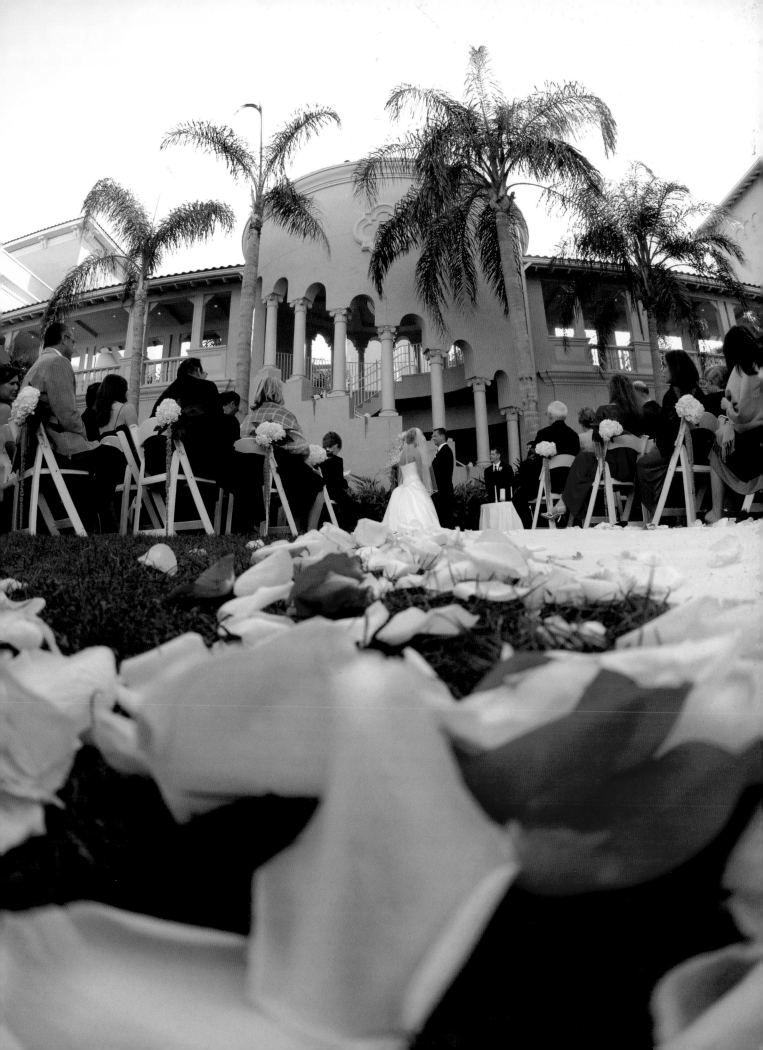

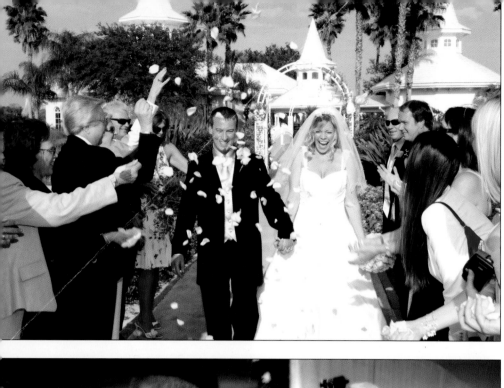

Top—The flower-petal toss (or some other event to mark the couple's exit) is an easy-to-anticipate event that is sure to result in some great images. (CAMERA: Nikon D2X, ISO: 100, LENS: 17–55mm at 32mm, EXPOSURE: $\frac{1}{250}$ second at f/8.0)

Bottom—The coy expression on the bride's face makes this a truly memorable exit shot. (CAMERA: Nikon D2X, ISO: 700, LENS: 17–55mm at 17mm, EXPOSURE: $\frac{1}{30}$ second at f/5.6)

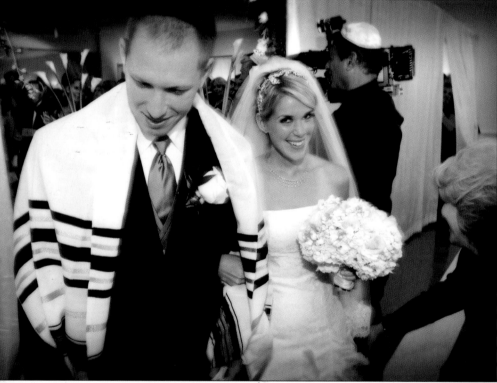

shots. This means you can move around more freely. Of course, you still do not want to linger in front of the parents or guests. Be as unobtrusive as possible. Constantly look for opportunities, then move in to execute them. Use your freedom of movement to its fullest, capturing all the little moments that make the wedding unique.

Exposure can be tricky at these outdoor venues—especially if you are working with the sun directly overhead. A good starting point is with the "Sunny 16 Rule." This states that in order to achieve a blue sky in your background, your exposure should be made with the aperture set to f/16 and the shutter speed set to the inverse of your ISO. For instance, if you are shooting at ISO 100, your exposure should be f/16 at $\frac{1}{100}$ second. This is just a reference and there are many other factors at work. However, it works as a good rule of thumb.

IF YOU ARE GOING TO INCORPORATE FILL FLASH, YOU SHOULD IDEALLY SHOOT WITH A LARGER APERTURE.

If you are going to incorporate fill flash, you should ideally shoot with a larger aperture such as f/8 or f/11. For most digital cameras, the flash sync speed is $\frac{1}{250}$ second, so that will limit how wide you can open your aperture. For example, if f/16 at $\frac{1}{100}$ second is the correct exposure at ISO 100, then a correlating correct exposure would be f/11 at $\frac{1}{200}$ second. We would typically take this shot at f/8.5 at $\frac{1}{250}$ second. Sometimes you might even drop your shutter speed down to $\frac{1}{125}$ second and sacrifice some of the blue in the sky for a better exposure of your subjects.

If the sun is in your lens, use it to your advantage. (**CAMERA:** Nikon D2Xs, **ISO:** 400, **LENS:** 17–55mm at 17mm, **EXPOSURE:** $\frac{1}{250}$ second at f/5)

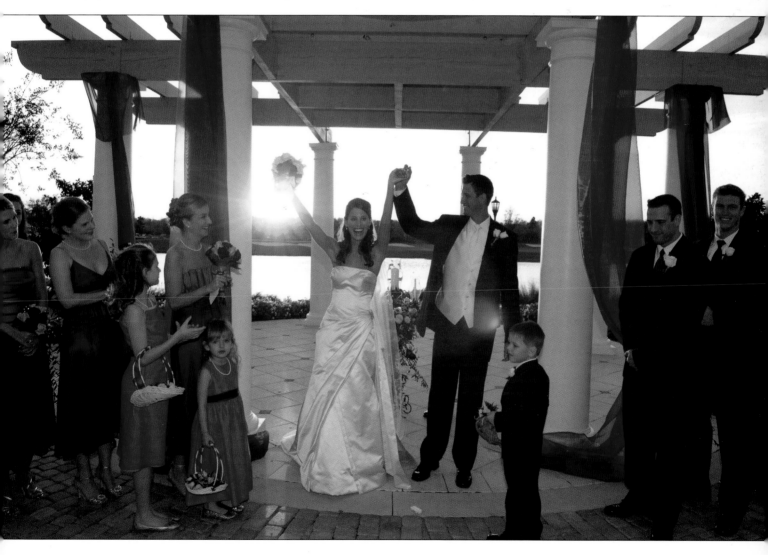

6. Family Shots and Posed Pictures

THEY PROBABLY WON'T END UP IN YOUR PORTFOLIO, but every couple wants at least a few family shots and posed pictures. Our studio feels that family shots are a very important part of the wedding day. In today's world, weddings are often one of the few times that all the family members are together in one place. It is important to document these moments for posterity. However, even though we feel family photos are important, we do not want to take all day with them. We would much rather spend time with the couple creating memorable images of them on

Group shots don't have to be stiff. This wedding party wanted to do a jumping shot. It might be a little cheesey, but we think it works. The image was enhanced with Kevin Kubota's Hawaiian Punch action, discussed in chapter 13. (CAMERA: Nikon D2Xs, ISO: 100, LENS: 10.5mm fisheye, EXPOSURE: $\frac{1}{250}$ second at f/8, LIGHTING: on-camera flash)

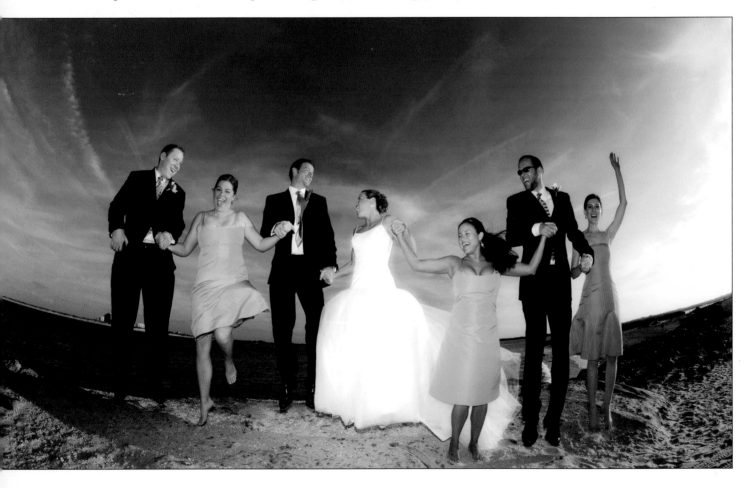

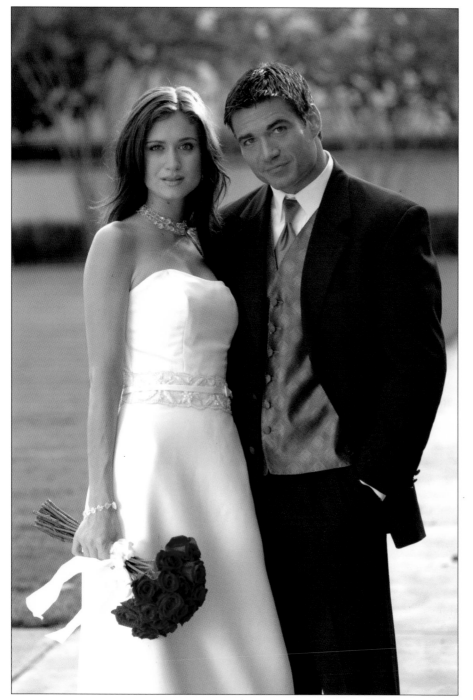

The basic L position is a good pose for a simple portrait, but it also forms the basis for quick group portraits. With the bride and groom in this position, the wedding party and family members can be arranged around them in whatever variations you like. (CAMERA: Nikon D2X, ISO: 100, LENS: 80–200mm at 92mm, EXPOSURE: ¹/₂₅₀ second at f/2.8)

their special day. Therefore, we try to steer the couple in this direction during their consultation.

BE EFFICIENT

After a typical church ceremony you will have thirty minutes to do photos before the wedding party needs to depart. And here's a little secret: The clock starts ticking when the couple kisses. When your thirty minutes are nearing their end, a mild-mannered church lady will hover over you looking at her watch and back at you. There may be a mass starting shortly or there may be another wedding (or she may just want to go home).

Here is how we maximize our allotted time. First, we pose the bride and groom in the L position (standing close with their feet at 90-degree angles and with their near arms around each other's backs) and ask them not to move. Then we add the celebrant. They are usually under a time constraint and ready to change out of their ceremonial clothing, so it makes sense to do this image right away.

Next, we work with the bride's parents, immediate family, and grandparents. If there are multiple sets of parents we try to call everyone by their first name. We also try to work quickly to avoid any awkwardness. In a parental divorce situation, this may be the first time the former spouses have been in the same room in a long while, so be sensitive. The bride and groom will more than likely inform you if there are any such "bad blood" situations.

Then, we switch to the groom's side and repeat the whole process. After that, we photograph the entire wedding party. Then we take a few shots of the bride and groom at the ceremony location. Afterwards, we will hopefully get twenty-five minutes with the bride and groom alone. We make this session short and sweet. We also inform the couple that we will be happy to photograph any extended family at the reception. This system works 95 percent of the time and clients seem to like it. You get the posed images that keep their parents happy, plus the more contemporary shots most brides and grooms prefer.

LIGHTING

To light your family shots, you have to make a decision between using on-camera flash or setting up strobes. The strobes will better illuminate dark areas and will afford you a greater depth of field. Your best exposure will probably be at f/8 at ISO 400. The downside is that strobes take time to set up and to break down. They can also be a liability if someone trips over a cord or knocks one over. It happens! If you think you have time, it is nice to use them. (*Note:* If you plan on using AC-powered strobes for lighting the big group shots, make sure you have located the power outlets prior to assembling the group.)

When the ambient lighting is low, on-camera flash can be used in the creation of your family shots. (**CAMERA:** Nikon D2Xs, **ISO:** 800, **LENS:** 50mm f/1.4, **EXPOSURE:** 1/60 second at f/4.5, **LIGHTING:** on-camera flash, **OTHER:** tripod)

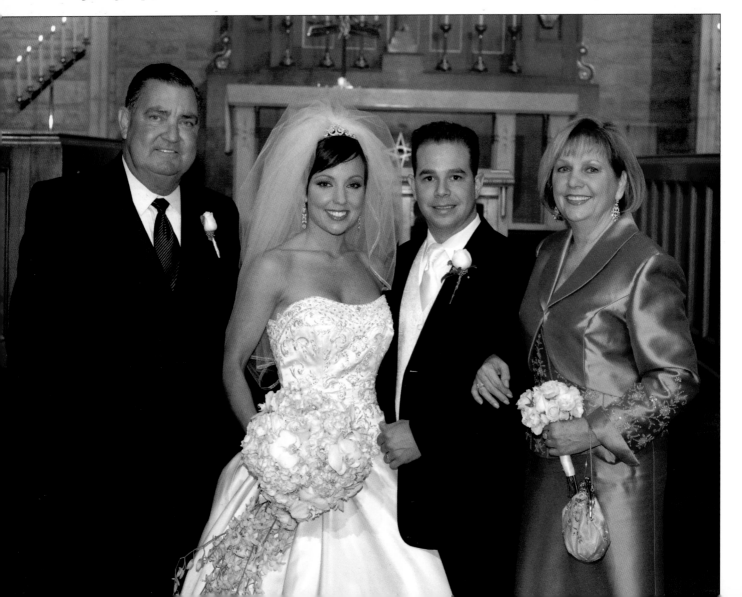

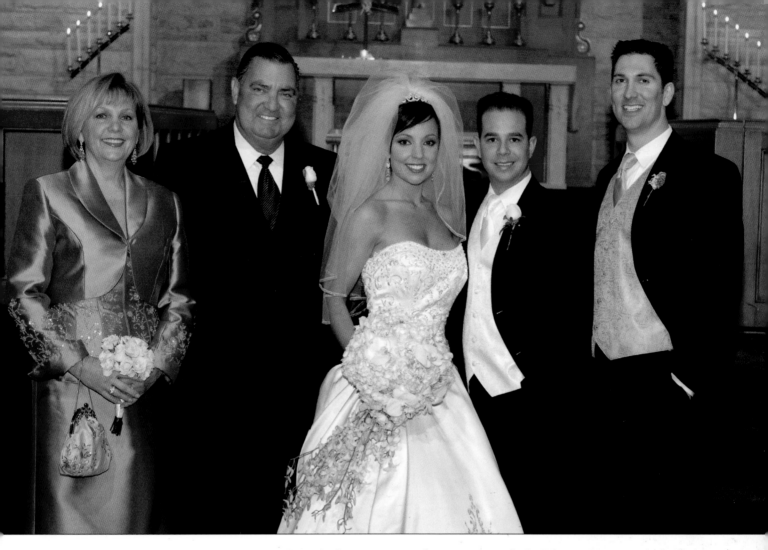

Maintaining order and control will help you execute the family portraits more efficiently. (**CAMERA:** Nikon D2Xs, **ISO:** 800, **LENS:** 50mm f/1.4, **EXPOSURE:** ¹⁄₆₀ second at f/4.5, **LIGHTING:** on-camera flash, **OTHER:** tripod)

In a pinch, you can employ on-camera flash. When using on-camera flash to light a group, we will often shoot at f/5.6 at ISO 800. We have made 20x30-inch prints from these files and they look good. Obviously, shooting at a lower ISO will yield a less noisy print. Unfortunately, this approach seems to be what the light requires in most of the churches we photograph.

LARGE GROUPS

Every once in a while you will encounter a big event where executing multiple large groups of family shots are necessary to close the deal. Don't fret. As long as you have ample time and a solid plan, it will work out fine. To execute large groups you need to have multiple levels. Churches tend to work nicely as they usually have steps.

Recently, we had a large family wedding that was held at a church. Because of time allotted, we were only able to do the immediate family shots at the church. However, big family photos were also extremely important for the mother of the bride. Serendipitously, we received permission to use a restaurant to execute these shots, which we were able to complete in just twenty minutes. Because we had it all coordinated and prescouted, and it came off without a hitch. Below is one shot from this session.

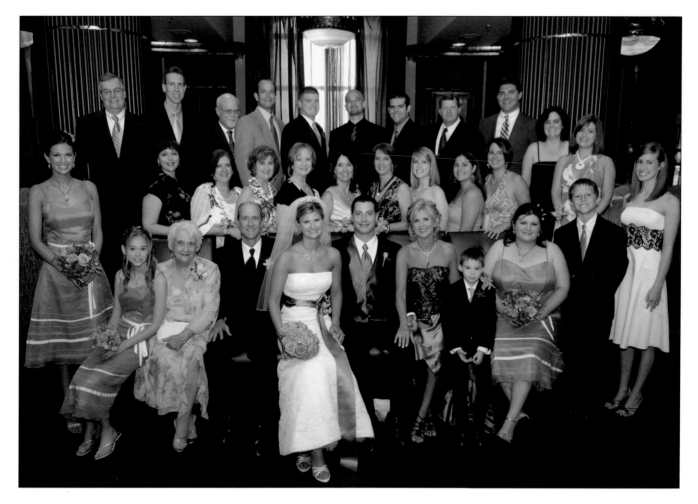

MAINTAIN CONTROL

When executing these family shots, you must remain in control. All too often with novice photographers, overzealous family members begin to "help." This is the kiss of death.

Typically we only have twenty-five to thirty minutes with the bride and groom alone, and each time Aunt Edna decides you should take a shot with another cousin or uncle or nephew, it eats into that time. Before you know it, they are ready to announce the bride and groom at the reception. The caterer, band, coordinator, and three hundred guests are all waiting and you have not created one nice portrait of the most important people at the event.

Wedding photographers need to pick their battles—and this is one you do not want to lose. Politely tell Aunt Edna that you will be happy to photograph all those family members at the reception, but right now it's critical that you get some wonderful shots of the bride and groom. This usually works and frees you to take the all-important money shots (see chapter 7).

When a big family shot is important to your clients (or their parents), planning and organization are the keys to success. (**CAMERA:** Nikon D2X, **ISO:** 800, **EXPOSURE:** $\frac{1}{30}$ second at f/5.6, **LIGHTING:** on-camera flash, **OTHER:** tripod)

7. The Money Shots

ETWEEN THE CEREMONY AND RECEPTION, you'll have some time to work with the bride and groom alone. We call these the "money shots," because these are the portraits that brides and grooms will invariably fall in love with and purchase. This is your opportunity to create images that will remind them why they hired you. In most cases, you'll only have about thirty minutes for this session, so work fast.

AT THE CHURCH

We typically start with a couple of shots at the ceremony venue—perhaps on the altar, if we're at a church. We do these quickly at the end of the wedding-party and family shots, because our thirty minutes of post-ceremony shooting time at the venue has usually expired at this point.

GOING OFF SITE

Once we have left the ceremony area and gotten rid of everyone else (including all those "helpers" like Aunt Edna) we can slow down and breathe—though we still only have thirty minutes, so there's no time to get too relaxed. If you must travel from the ceremony to the reception site, be mindful to negotiate extra time in the planning process to allow for this. Generally we do not

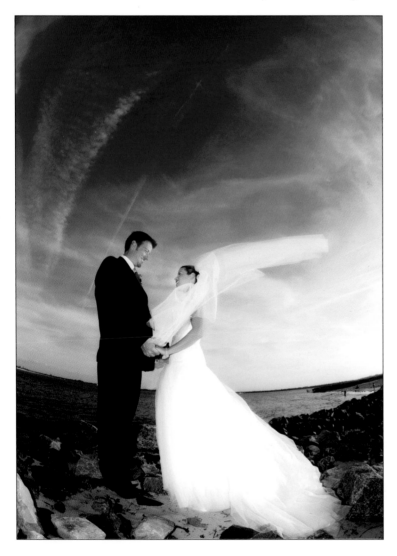

When working on location with the bride and groom, keep an eye out for veil-lifting winds. (**CAMERA:** Nikon D2Xs, **ISO:** 100, **LENS:** 10.5mm fisheye, **EXPOSURE:** 1/250 second at f/8, **LIGHTING:** on-camera flash)

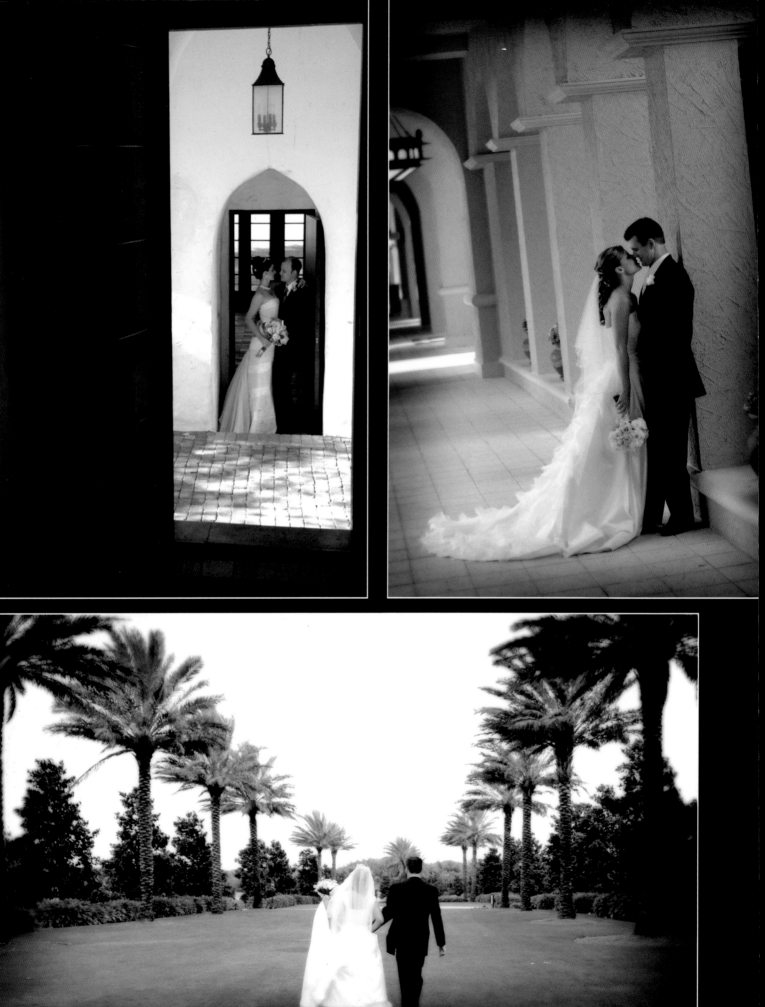

Facing Page, Top Left—Using the doorway to frame the couple makes it feel as though we are being given a glimpse into a private moment. (CAMERA: Nikon D2X, ISO: 200, LENS: 17–55mm at 32mm, EXPOSURE: ¹/₁₆₀ second at f/2.8)

Facing Page, Top Right—A shot of the couple kissing is always romantic. (CAMERA: Nikon D2Xs, ISO: 400, LENS: 50mm f/1.4, EXPOSURE: ¹/₁₂₅ second at f/3.5)

Facing Page, Bottom—A photograph of the bride and groom walking away from the camera makes a nice transition shot. (CAMERA: Nikon D2Xs, ISO: 320, LENS: 17–55mm at 17mm, EXPOSURE: ¹/₂₀₀ second at f/5.6)

The bride's coy expression as she received a kiss from her new husband makes this shot a winner. (CAMERA: Nikon D2X, ISO: 800, LENS: 50mm f/1.4, EXPOSURE: ¹/₁₂₅ second at f/6.3)

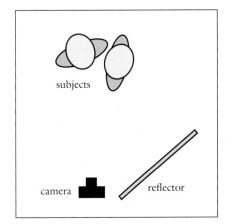

venture too far from the wedding and/or reception site. Instead, we make the most out of our environment.

When we leave the ceremony site, we look for little kissy moments and record the bride and groom walking from behind. We work around the lighting and do a few closer portraits. We encourage closeness with our posing. We may also do additional bridal portraits, since we do not have the restraints we did before the wedding, such as worries about people seeing the bride before the ceremony and/or marring the dress. This does not mean we will

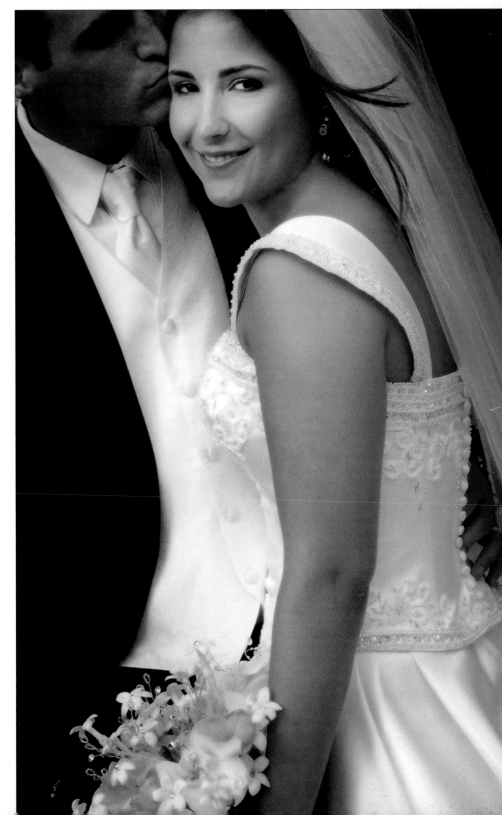

trash the dress, but brides are much less concerned about it at this time. This allows us to try more poses and be more adventurous with our shooting.

FINDING BACKGROUNDS

When creating these photographs, take advantage of everything in the surrounding environment. Do not slip into the tunnel vision some photographers develop when they put the camera up to their eye. Train your peripheral vision and know what is going on around you at all times. You must really im-

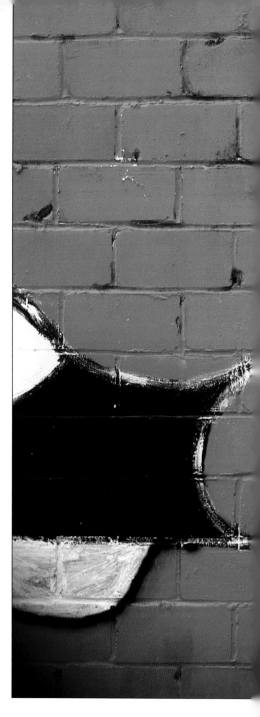

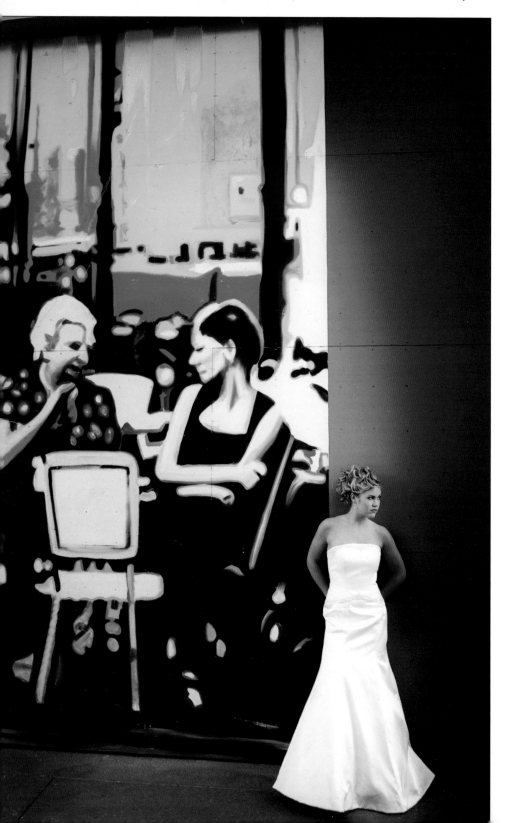

A popular trend recently has been photographing brides against very saturated, colorful backgrounds. Here, the ladies in the mural also made for an interesting composition. (**CAMERA:** Nikon D2X, **ISO:** 200, **LENS:** 17–55mm f/2.8 at 17mm, **EXPOSURE:** $\frac{1}{250}$ second at f/2.8)

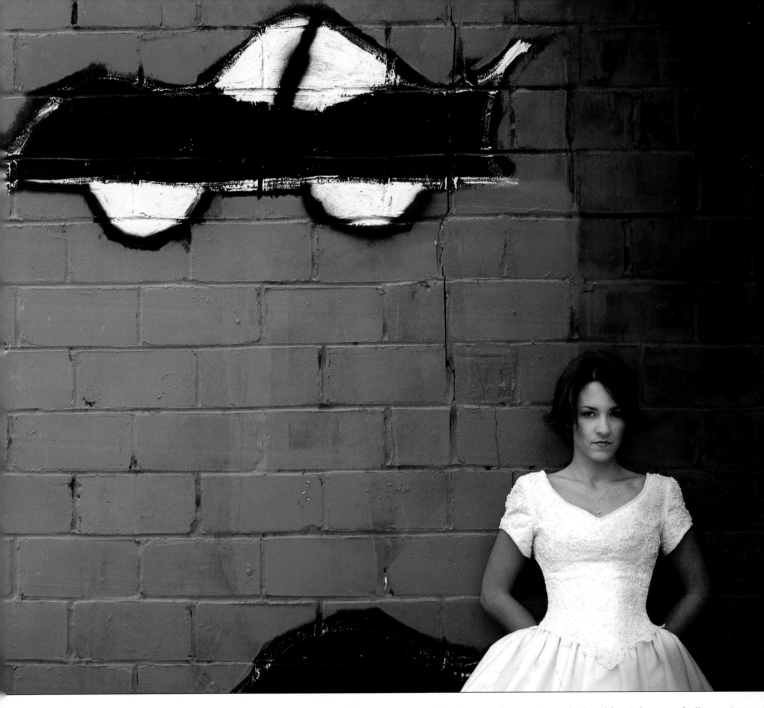

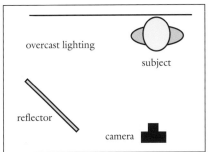

The bride is juxtaposed against bright graffiti for a very contemporary look. (**CAMERA:** Nikon D1X, **ISO:** 320, **LENS:** 50mm f/1.4, **EXPOSURE:** 1/400 second at f/4.5)

merse yourself to come up with the goods consistently (and by "the goods," I mean better-than-average photographs). In the competitive market of wedding photography, this is what you must produce to survive.

During this session, we employ simple but classic techniques. We also love to juxtapose things in unexpected ways, like picturing the bride next to a downtown mural or Harley-Davidson sign. The only rules you have to follow are making images that your clients will love. We try to incorporate fashion and photojournalism, consistently looking for moments that happen naturally. However, we are not afraid to set up a great shot. To keep things moving quickly, we usually work with one camera, a tripod if the light is low,

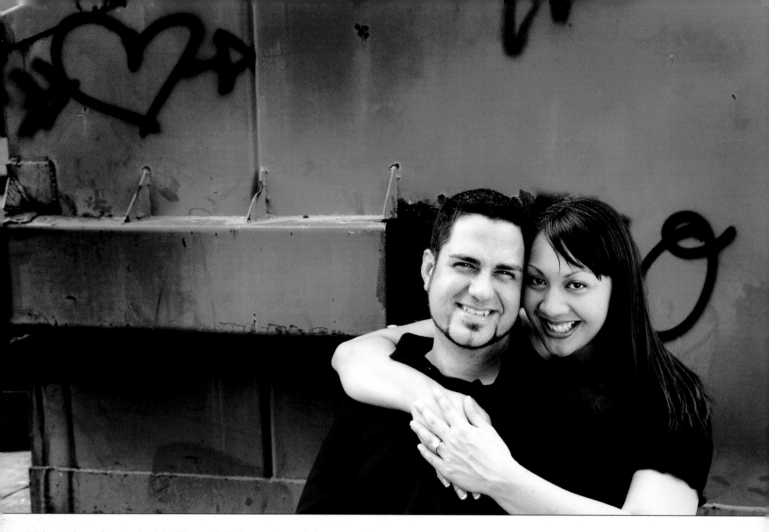

three lenses (a 24–70mm f/2.8, a 16mm fisheye, and an 80–200mm f/2.8), and a reflector.

Some locations are fabulously clean and beautiful. Other aren't—in fact, a lot of sites downtown near our studio are downright grungy. To adapt, we've learned to maximize the good things and minimize the bad. During his seminars, Tony Corbell often shows a beautiful portrait with an out-of-focus green-blue background. The next slide is a wider shot that reveals that the background was really a dumpster. It just goes to show that beautiful backgrounds are everywhere if you know how to use the scenes around you. It is all in how you look at things; if life gives you lemons, make lemonade.

TWILIGHT

During the post-ceremony portrait session, we try to capitalize on available light, especially if we are lucky enough to be working with twilight. This is our favorite part of the day.

Twilight typically happens about ten minutes after the sun goes down. Unlike sunsets, which are not very consistent, twilight is very consistent. It is the cool midnight blue that lasts about seven to ten minutes. We believe

The vibrant background for this couple's portrait was actually a graffiti-covered dumpster. (CAMERA: Nikon D2X, ISO: 320, LENS: 17–55mm at 26mm, EXPOSURE: 1/250 second at f/4)

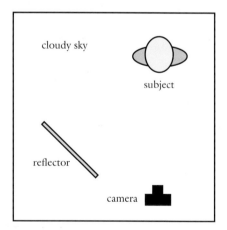

Facing Page—This striking bridal portrait is a study in color and saturation. (CAMERA: Nikon D2X, ISO: 100, LENS: 17–55mm at 20mm, EXPOSURE: 1/200 second at f/6.3)

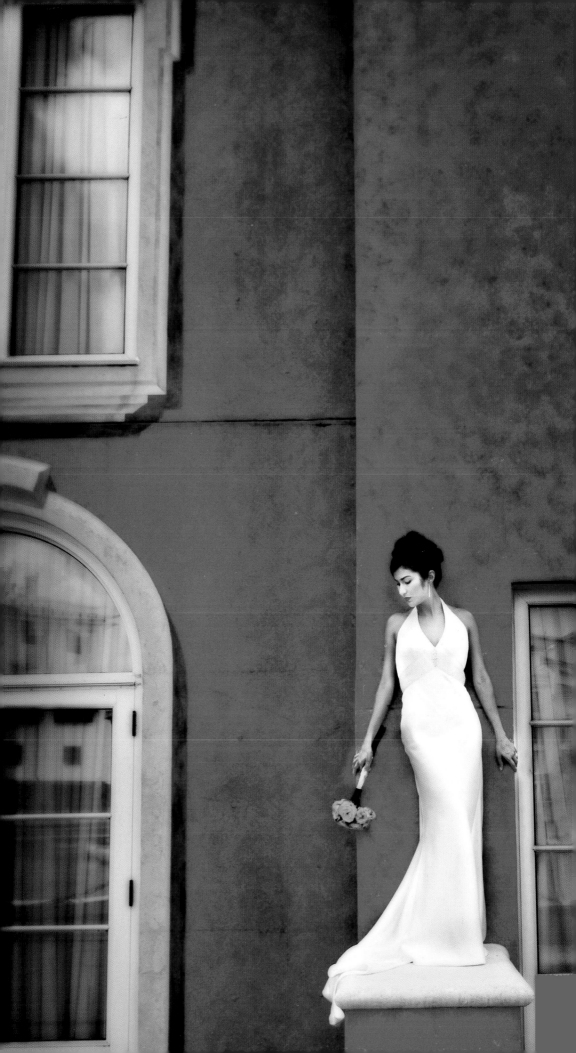

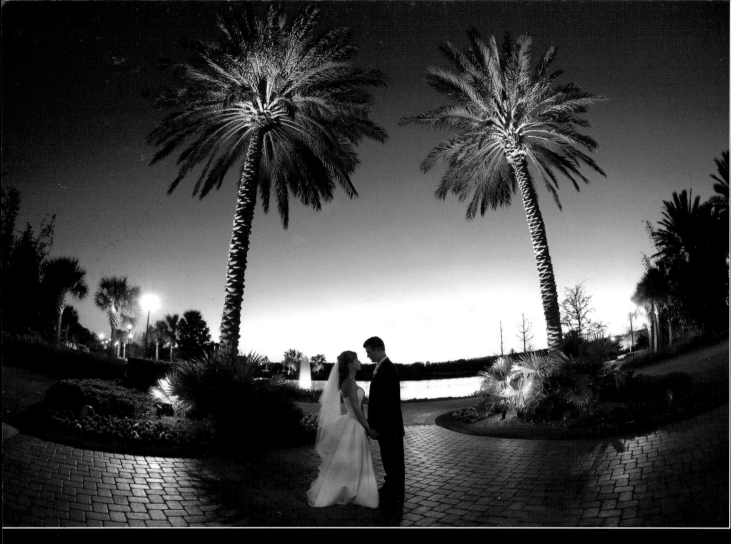

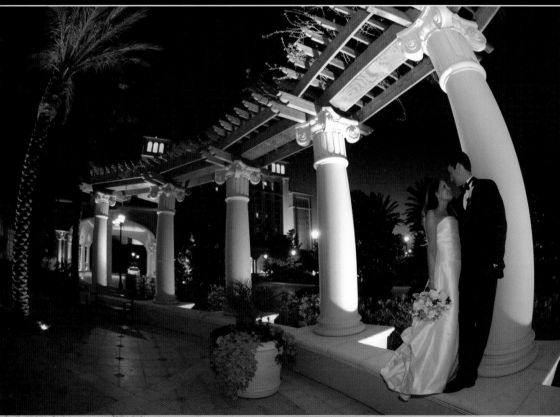

Above—Capturing twilight requires some good timing—but it's well worth the effort. (CAMERA: Nikon D2Xs, ISO: 800, LENS: 10.5mm fisheye, EXPOSURE: ½ second at f/4, OTHER: tripod)

Left—Architectural lighting complements the twilight in the portrait, which was created with just a touch of fill flash on the subjects. (CAMERA: Nikon D2Xs, ISO: 800, LENS: 10.5mm fisheye, EXPOSURE: ⅙ second at f/2.8, LIGHTING: fill flash set ½ stop below ambient light reading, OTHER: tripod)

Facing Page—This well-lit venue and fountain provided the perfect setting for a nice twilight silhouette. (CAMERA: Nikon D100, ISO: 800, LENS: 16mm, EXPOSURE: ¼₀ second at f/2.8, WHITE BALANCE: tungsten, OTHER: tripod)

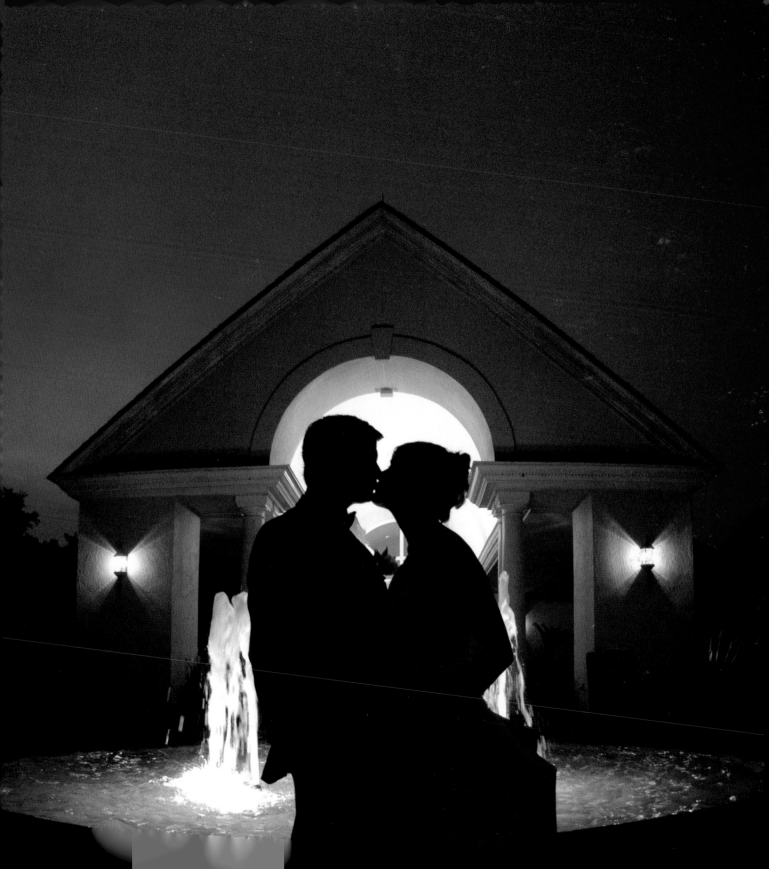

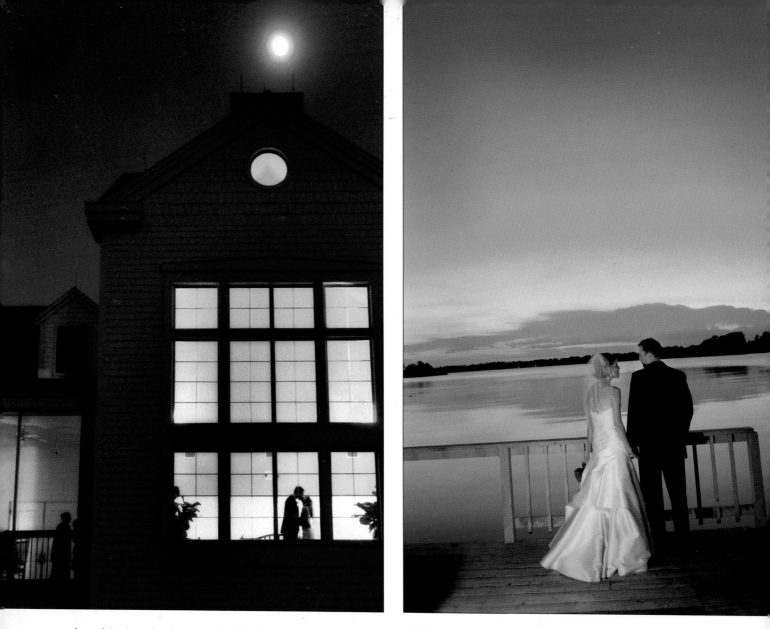

that this time looks great in the digital format. Twilight is a romantic time and if you execute these shots correctly you can really set yourself apart from the pack. (*Note:* Typically, we check online so we know ahead of time when sunset will occur. More often than not, twilight occurs after the reception has started. If this is the case, we let the bride and groom get introduced, eat a little something, and then pull them outside for about five to seven minutes for a quick shoot.)

After the money shots are in the can, the bride gets bustled and we run in to document the next part of our journey.

Room Shots Before the Reception

Room shots are very important. Whether it is a million-dollar wedding or an event of a much smaller scale, a lot of thought went into the reception room and it is imperative to document it properly. The challenge is that most rooms

Left—The blues were saturated in postproduction to give this twilight portrait a very graphic look. (CAMERA: Nikon D2X, ISO: 800, LENS: 17–55mm at 26mm, EXPOSURE: ½ second at f/2.8, OTHER: tripod)

Right—Twilight from behind the subjects was given an extra punch with a videographer's light to camera left. (CAMERA: Nikon D2Xs, ISO: 800, LENS: 17–55mm at 17mm, EXPOSURE: ⅓ second at f/2.8, LIGHTING: twilight and videographer's light, OTHER: tripod)

Right—An intense spotlight illuminated this cake. Adding on-camera flash helped balance this for a more appealing image. (**CAMERA:** Nikon D2X, **ISO:** 800, **LENS:** 17–55mm at 26mm, **EXPOSURE:** 1/50 second at f/4, **LIGHTING:** on-camera flash, **OTHER:** tripod)

Below—These favors were handmade by the mother for the reception, so it was critical to document them. (**CAMERA:** Nikon D2Xs, **ISO:** 800, **LENS:** 17–55mm at 17mm, **EXPOSURE:** 1/3 second at f/2.8, **LIGHTING:** twilight and videographer's light, **OTHER:** tripod)

Bottom—The Fort Myers Convention Center was transformed into an elegant reception room for the six hundred guests attending this wedding. Showing the cake in the foreground really sets the stage. (**CAMERA:** Nikon D2X, **ISO:** 800, **LENS:** 17–55mm at 17mm, **EXPOSURE:** 1/3 second at f/5.6, **OTHER:** tripod)

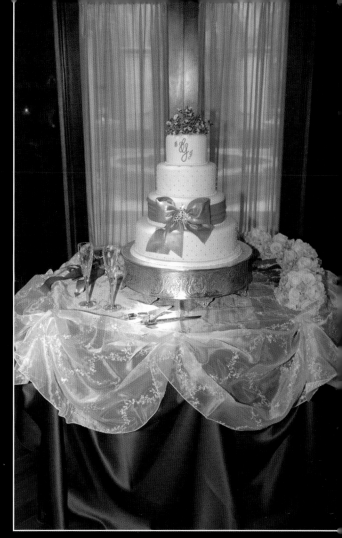

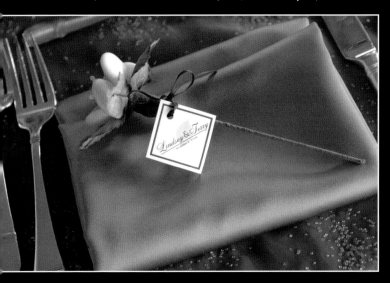

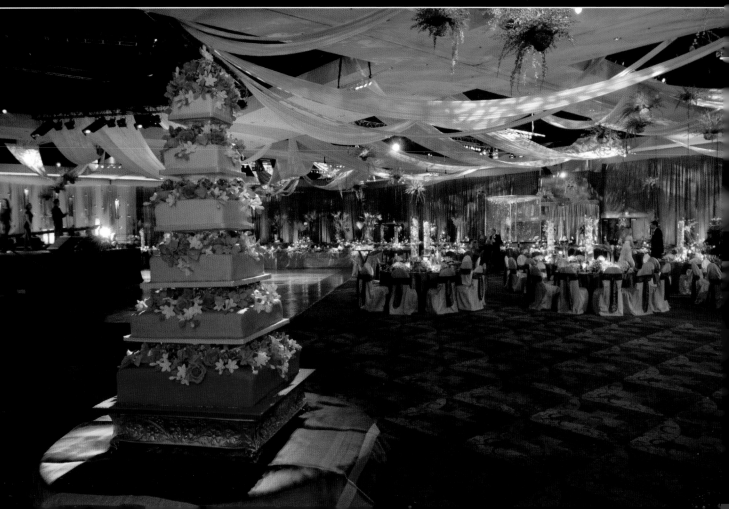

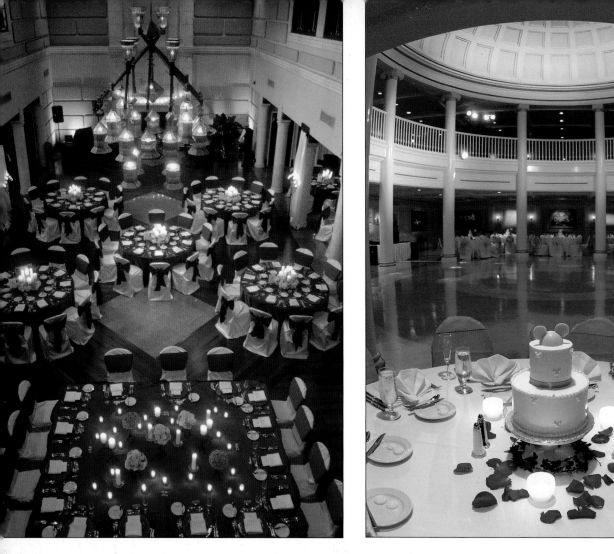

are ready only moments before the guests are prepared to be seated. Candles are lit, final touches are made, and there is frenetic activity everywhere. You have servers, florists, and coordinators in your way—and you are the last thing they care about as they are trying to set up a stunning room. If you're lucky, you will get about three minutes with the room perfect. If you have befriended the banquet captain or hotel manager, you may get the servers out of your shot. (In the old days, photographers would yell and tell everyone to get out of their shot, but that is generally frowned upon today.)

This is our strategy for starting the shooting when we arrive at the reception venue. If there is activity all over the room, shoot the details. Do not waste time! Capture cakes, plates, menus, and tables. Photograph the favor the bride's mother made and the handkerchief the groom's grandmother embroidered. All of these little details tell the story. We do most of this shooting with available light on a tripod. Then, we shoot individual place settings, groups of tables, and sides of the room.

When you're done, ask the appropriate gatekeeper (banquet captain or service manager) if you can have the room cleared for three minutes before

Left—This image of the reception venue, Isleworth Country Club, was photographed from the balcony one minute before the doors opened. (CAMERA: Nikon D70, ISO: 800, LENS: 17–55mm at 20mm, EXPOSURE: ¹⁄₁₅ second at f/2.8, OTHER: tripod)

Right—Symmetry is the hallmark of this reception shot, photographed at Epcot's American Adventure. (CAMERA: Nikon D1X, ISO: 800, LENS: 16mm, EXPOSURE: ¹⁄₄ second at f/2.8, OTHER: tripod)

Facing Page, Top—As these complex centerpieces show, no small amount of work goes into the planning and preparation of the reception. (CAMERA: Nikon D2Xs, ISO: 800, LENS: 17–55mm at 26mm, EXPOSURE: ¹⁄₂ second at f/5.6, OTHER: tripod)

Facing Page, Bottom—Shooting a timed release from a tripod allows you to capture the incredible lighting in many reception venues. (CAMERA: Nikon D2X, ISO: 800, LENS: 17–55mm at 17mm, EXPOSURE: ¹⁄₃ second at f/5.6, OTHER: tripod)

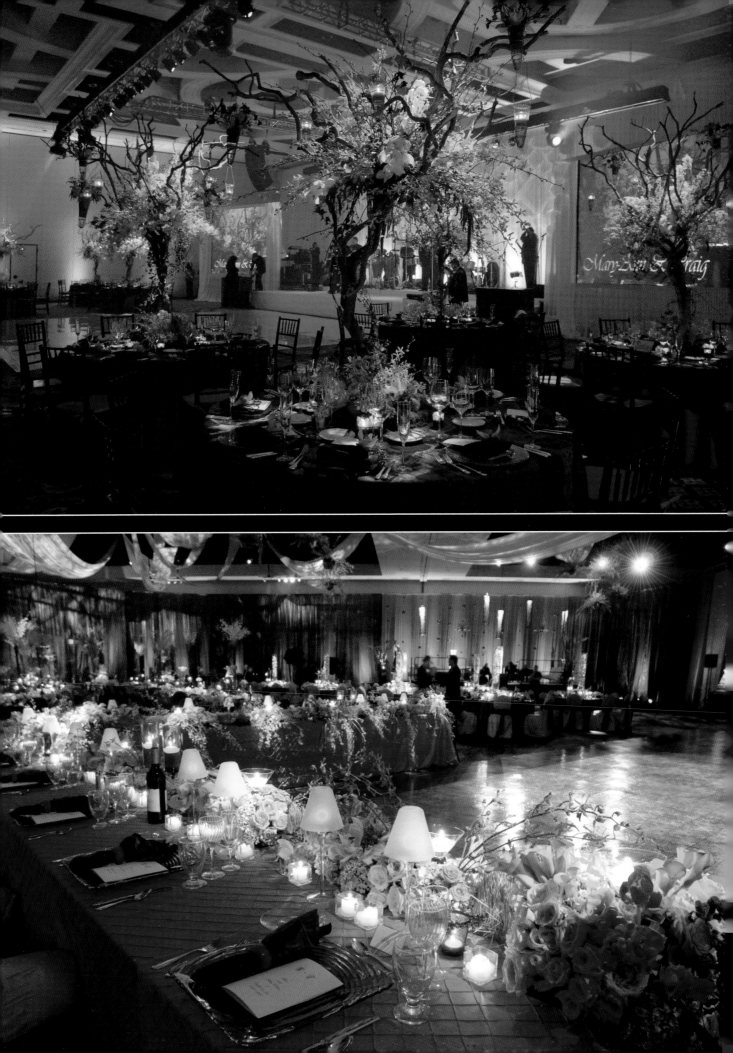

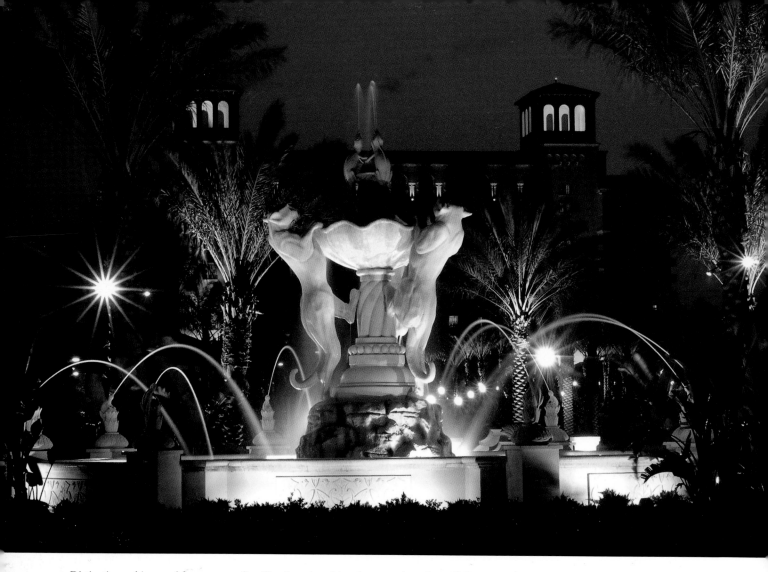

Distinctive architectural features are often illuminated, making them stand out beautifully against a twilight sky. A small aperture was used to maximize the depth of field in this shot, which would make a great transition shot in the couple's album. (**CAMERA:** Nikon D1X, ISO: 800, **LENS:** 17–55mm at 20mm, **EXPOSURE:** 20 seconds at f/20, **OTHER:** tripod)

they open the doors. You may also want to ask them to adjust the lighting a little. Begin your shooting with the widest shots—the staff will begin walking back in at any second and you may have to shoot around them. We usually start with a fisheye and then get tighter from there. We use a tripod and employ the timed shutter release on the camera. This helps ensure a steady sharp photograph.

Once you have the inside documented, don't forget the outside of the venue. Twilight shots of the venue are very dynamic and really help the album flow. And make sure to solidify your relationships with the venue managers by providing them with images of their facilities. If you follow up with these folks after the event, the next time you work at their venue they will make your job much easier.

TWILIGHT SHOTS OF THE VENUE ARE VERY DYNAMIC AND REALLY HELP THE ALBUM FLOW.

8. The Reception

THE PARTY IS ON! Just when you thought it was time to relax, it's time for the reception. Hopefully by now you have captured all the necessary room shots (see chapter 7). If not, there is nothing that says you can't do them with people in the frame. At most weddings, the reception starts with you and the guests in the reception room waiting for the bridal party to be announced.

BEFORE THE COUPLE ARRIVES

Before the couple makes their entrance, we try to find a good place to stash our gear that is both accessible but out of the way of servers, guests, bartenders, and other venue staff. A remote corner of the room usually works.

While you're waiting for the bride and groom to be announced, room shots with the guests can be created. (CAMERA: Nikon D2Xs, ISO: 800, LENS: 10.5mm fisheye, EXPOSURE: 1/3 second at f/4, OTHER: tripod)

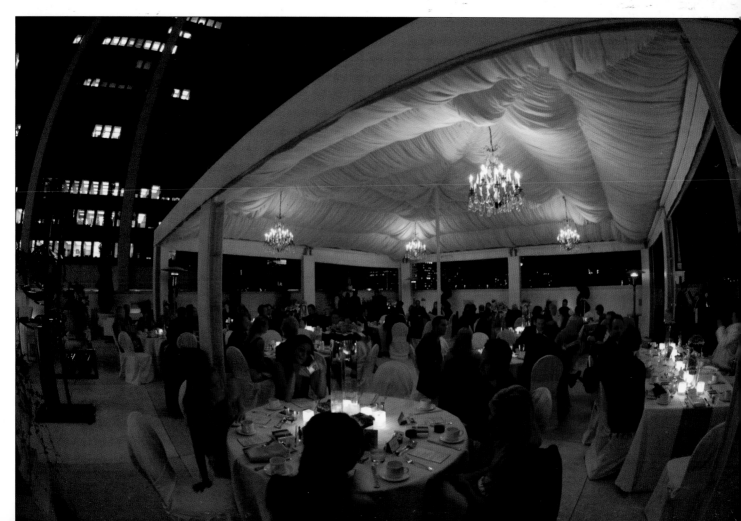

Remember to keep all bags zipped up just in case any helpful hotel staffers try to move it for you. Next, we touch base with the DJ to go over the schedule of events.

Before the couple arrives, we look for fun expressions on the guests' faces and document any crazy behavior as the party gets started. We generally shoot these candids at ISO 800, exposing at anywhere from f/5.6 at $\frac{1}{50}$ second down to f/4 at $\frac{1}{15}$ second. For these images, we usually shoot with a 17–35mm f/2.8, a 24–70mm, or a fisheye lens.

ARRIVALS

Next come the announcements marking the arrival of the bride and groom (or, in some cases, the entire wedding party). The key shot here is the bride and groom entering. We will usually photograph everyone in the wedding party who is announced, but we really want a nice one of the bride and groom. Using a two-photographer system, we like to capture this shot from both the front and the back.

THE FIRST DANCE

Once the announcements occur, the bride and groom usually go right into the first dance. When photographing this, we try to capture a nice wide establishing shot as well as some tighter shots showing the emotion of the mo-

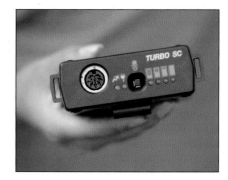

Using the Quantum Turbo SC will enable the AA batteries in your flash to last forever and eliminate recycle time. We would not do a wedding without them.

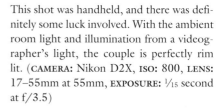

This shot was handheld, and there was definitely some luck involved. With the ambient room light and illumination from a videographer's light, the couple is perfectly rim lit. (CAMERA: Nikon D2X, ISO: 800, LENS: 17–55mm at 55mm, EXPOSURE: $\frac{1}{15}$ second at f/3.5)

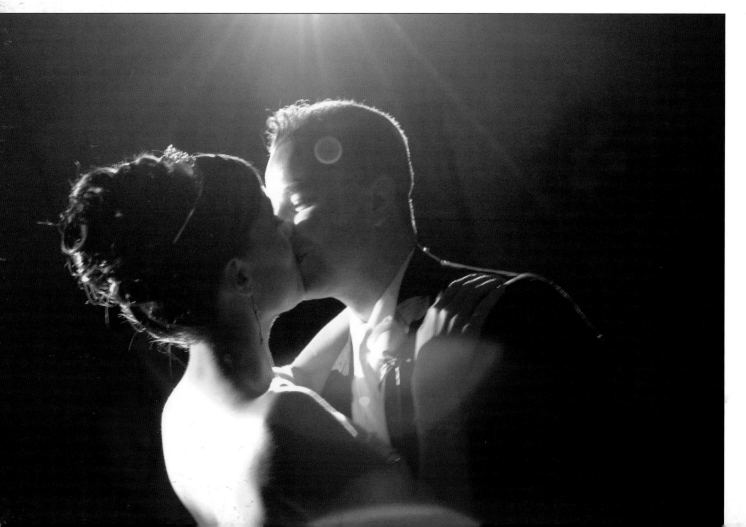

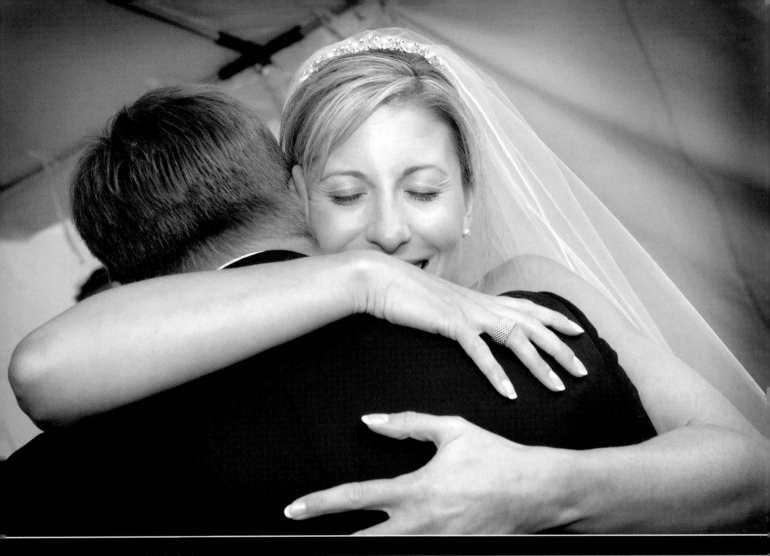

Above—Emotions run high during the first dance. (**CAMERA**: Nikon D2Xs, **ISO**: 400, **LENS**: 17–55mm at 40mm, **EXPOSURE**: $\frac{1}{250}$ second at f/6.3, **LIGHTING**: on-camera flash)

Right—Take your time when photographing the first dance—there will be numerous opportunities to capture intimate moments. (**CAMERA**: Nikon D2Xs, **ISO**: 800, **LENS**: 17–55mm at 55mm, **EXPOSURE**: $\frac{1}{50}$ second at f/4, **LIGHTING**: on-camera flash)

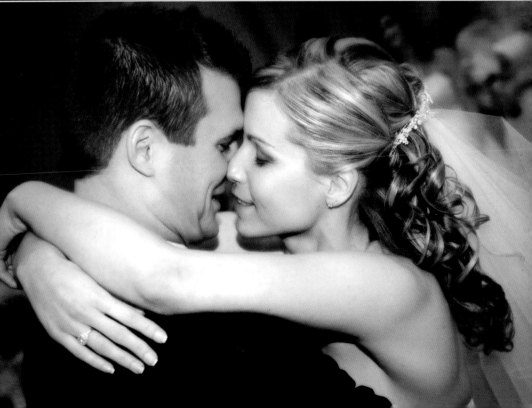

ment. You will have plenty of time to achieve both, so relax and tune in to your surroundings. In addition to the shots of the bride and groom, do not overlook reaction shots of the parents, bridal party, family, and guests. These can be priceless and make smooth transitions for the album.

The Toasts

Next are the toasts. We shoot these from two different angles, covering both the toasters and toastees. Then we capture them all together. Again, do not linger in front of the guests; they did not come there to see your backside. Move in, get your shot, and move out. Zero in on reactions—especially those of the parents and family. Look for tears, smiles, and laughter. It's all about emotion, emotion, emotion.

A Quick Break (and Some Makeup Shots)

When the toasts are completed, the photographers may get a little break. Once the guests are started on their dinners, the venue will typically have vendor meals available in the back of the facility. It may be tempting to take a load off and chow down, but the savvy photographer will not rest just yet.

Do not linger in front of the guests; they did not come there to see your backside.

Be sure to capture not just those giving the toasts, but also the reactions to their words. (CAMERA: Nikon D2X, ISO: 800, LENS: 17–55mm at 55mm, EXPOSURE: 1/40 second at f/4, LIGHTING: on-camera flash)

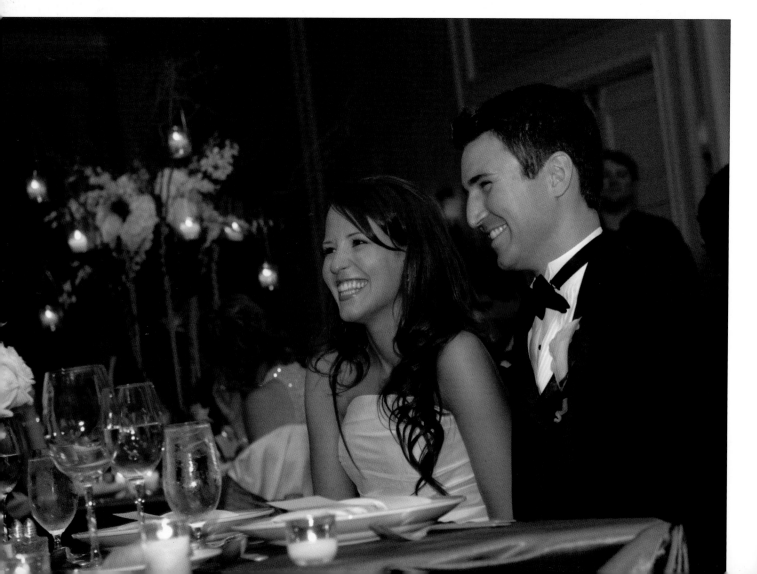

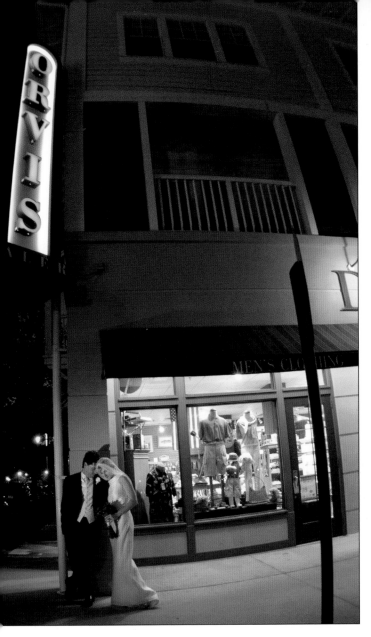

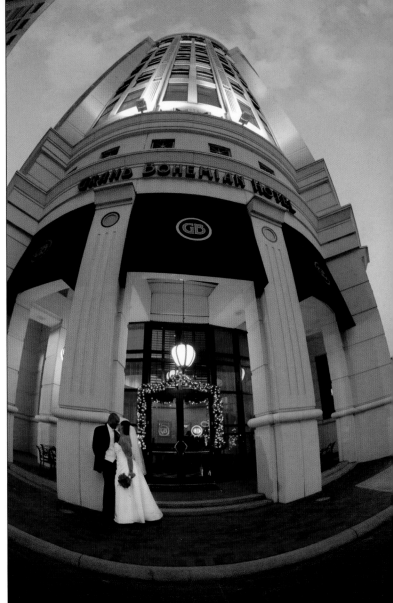

Left—Too late for a twilight image? Night-scapes, particularly in urban environments, can be equally dramatic. (CAMERA: Nikon D2Xs, ISO: 800, LENS: 16mm, EXPOSURE: 1/8 second at f/4, OTHER: tripod)

Right—If you can steal the bride and groom away for a few minutes while the guests are eating, it's a great time to photograph them outside the venue. (CAMERA: Nikon D2Xs, ISO: 800, LENS: 10.5mm fisheye, EXPOSURE: 1/20 second at f/2.8, OTHER: tripod)

This is the time to make up anything you might have missed in the whirlwind you just experienced. Get that cake shot you skipped or capture the twilight shot of the outside of the venue. Make sure your gear is in order. Only then should you go check on the plates they have waiting for you in the back.

TRY FOR TWILIGHT SHOTS

At this time, we decide if we want to pull the bride and groom aside for a twi-light or a nightscape shot. The bride and groom usually eat first and then mingle with their guests, so there is a brief opportunity to pull them away for this shot. We work fast, trying to get these shots done in less than ten min-utes. If the bride and groom are gone from the reception for very long, it dis-rupts the flow of the party. Remember that everyone there has an agenda, including the DJ, the caterer, the venue manager, and the coordinator. If

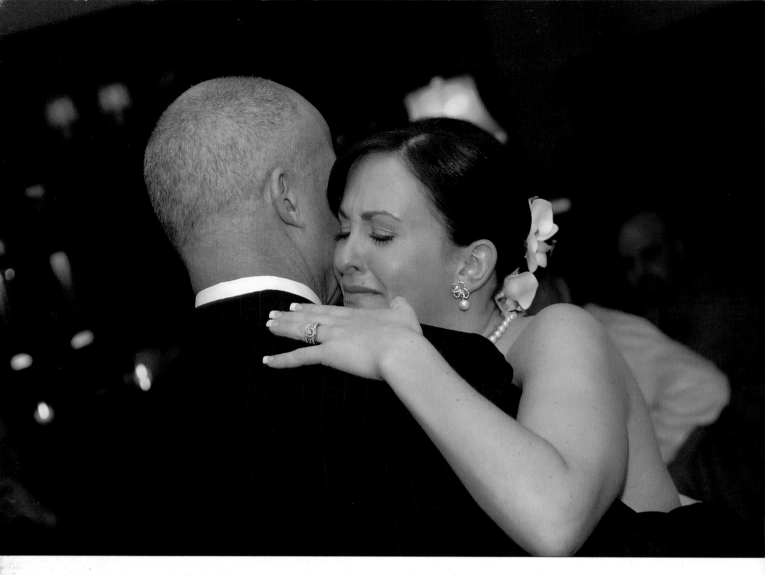

you disappear with the bride and groom for too long, it really can hurt the timing of the reception.

If you decide to execute these shots, go out and scout your locations while the bride and groom are eating. Test an exposure using your assistant as the subject. Then, when you are ready, you can just plug the bride and groom into the shot and get them right back to the party.

The parent dances typically come after dinner and can be quite filled with emotion. (CAMERA: Nikon D2Xs, ISO: 800, LENS: 17–55mm at 55mm, EXPOSURE: $\frac{1}{50}$ second at f/4, LIGHTING: on-camera flash)

PARENT DANCES

After dinner—and hopefully you did get to choke down something to eat— the parent dances start. This is an excellent time to get some really emotional shots. Key in on the father–daughter dance. There are often tears here. Be ready for a kiss on the cheek at the end of the song.

THE PARTY GETS STARTED

After the parent dances, the real party begins. We like to have fun with the guests, but also we watch the bride and groom like Labrador retrievers. If they make eye contact like they want a photo with some friends, we are right there. We also stalk the dance floor looking for interesting shots. We look for different perspectives and never stay in one place too long. We like to climb up on chairs or DJ speakers and shoot over the crowd using wide-angle or fisheye lenses. (Do Hail Mary shots like this at your own risk—if you fall off a speaker you will be the talk of the industry for a few weeks!)

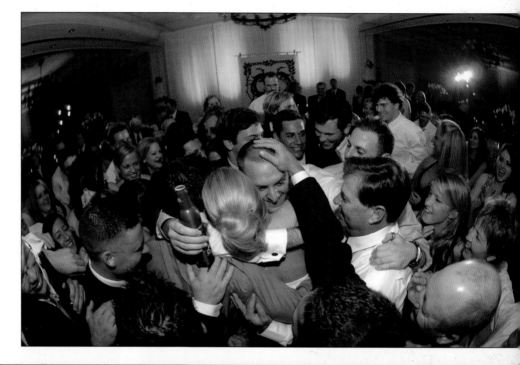

Right—A shot like this is a Hail Mary effort—but if it works, the results can be wonderful. (CAMERA: Nikon D2Xs, ISO: 800, LENS: 10.5mm fisheye, EXPOSURE: 1/40 second at f/4, LIGHTING: on-camera flash)

Left—The party is definitely on in this available light shot. (CAMERA: Nikon D200, ISO: 800, LENS: 10.5mm fisheye, EXPOSURE: 1/30 second at f/2.8, OTHER: tripod)

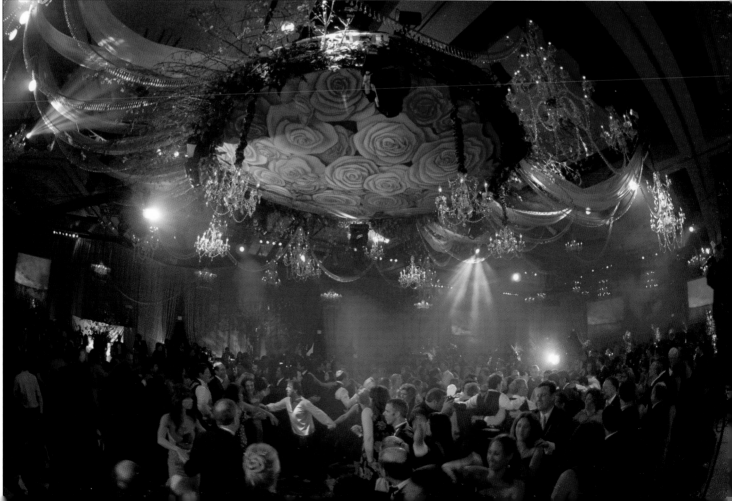

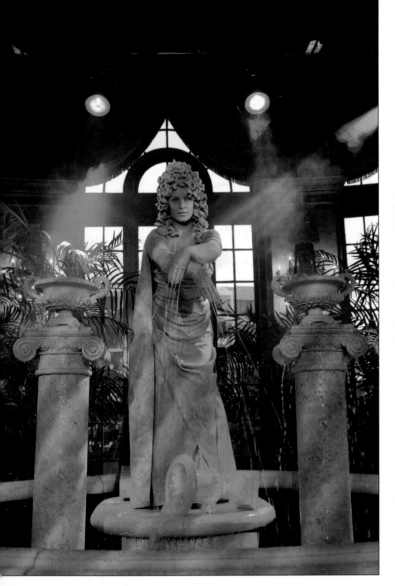

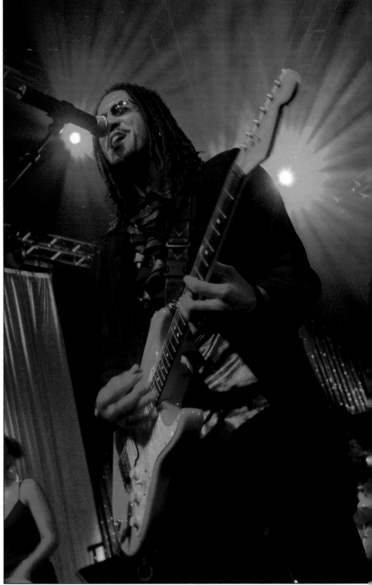

As the party progresses, people lose their inhibitions and you can get some crazy shots. However, do not lose your awareness of everything else happening around you. Just because you are in the mosh pit, do not overlook the grandmother saying goodbye as she leaves. It is your job to capture everything; to do so you have to increase your awareness.

The couple will have carefully chosen the night's entertainment, so make sure to include the performers in your coverage. Shoot with available light only to preserve the dramatic lighting; flash will wash it out. (CAMERA: Nikon D2X, ISO: 800, LENS: 24mm)

CAKE CUTTING

Besides the fun and dancing, there are a few key aspects of the reception left, including the cake cutting, the bouquet and garter tosses, and the grand exit. We usually document the cake cutting at f/4 for $\frac{1}{40}$ or $\frac{1}{60}$ second. Make sure you have the best vantage point for the shot. Wedding goers are often a little inebriated at this point and do not mind jumping in front of you. Just politely remind them that you are here photographing for the bride and groom. That usually does the trick.

In the old days, there was an exact pose for the cake cutting. You had the groom farthest away from you on the right side of the cake. The couple would put their arms around each other and hold the knife with their outside hands. This would show off the bride's ring.

These days, our studio goes with the flow. We just let it happen. If the couple asks us to pose them, we will do so in the aforementioned manner. However, we prefer to just document at this point. The bride and groom are adults who are capable of cutting a cake—and if they are *not* posed, we might be able to capture a more natural, genuine moment. Also, be ready for the cake smash. It does not happen a lot, but when it does, it can make for some exciting photographs.

> IF THEY ARE NOT POSED,
> WE MIGHT BE ABLE TO CAPTURE
> A MORE NATURAL, GENUINE MOMENT.

GARTER AND BOUQUET TOSSES
The next events are the garter and bouquet tosses. The DJ will ask someone for a chair and the bride will sit. Then he will play some bawdy music while the groom removes the garter. This can make for some funny shots. Watch, at the end, for the garter to inevitably end up in the groom's mouth.

This is a fun cake-cutting shot that captures the spirit of the moment. (**CAMERA:** Nikon D2Xs, **ISO:** 800, **LENS:** 17–55mm at 32mm, **EXPOSURE:** 1/40 second at f/4)

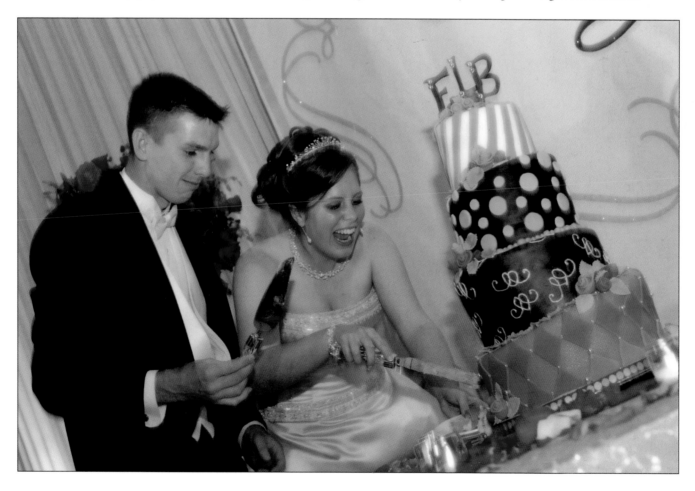

Next, all the single ladies line up, and the bride throws the bouquet. Using our two-photographer system, one of us photographs the bride throwing the bouquet and the other photographs the single girls trying to catch it. If you are by yourself, you can capture a wide shot from the side that includes both the throw and the catch. Timing is everything; you will probably only get one shot.

After the bouquet toss, all the single guys line up and we repeat the process with the groom tossing the garter. Sometimes we also get the groom with the garter before he throws it.

Once we have the people who caught the bouquet and garter, the DJ sometimes brings back the chair and has the woman who caught the bouquet sit in it. The gentleman who caught the garter will now be instructed to place it on her leg. The DJ will usually give him some instructions to the effect that every inch he places the garter above the knee will be seven years good luck for the bride and groom. It is nice if the bride and groom are standing behind the newly formed couple while this is taking place. These shots are a lot of fun, and with the bride and groom behind them you can incorporate their reactions as well.

BACK TO THE PARTY

After this frivolity, the party is back on. During this time, we do not mind getting people together for "happy face shots." These photos always work in the album, and the guests seem to love doing them. We just ask people to lean together and then click. Other things to look for are the bride and groom or family members playing with the band, surprise an-

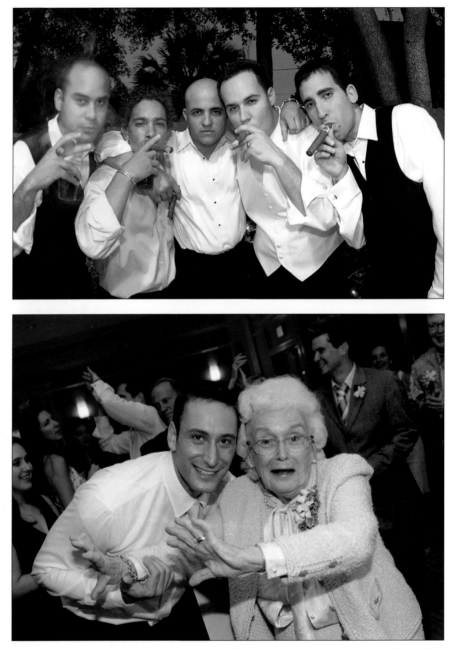

Pictures of people having fun at the reception always work great in the couple's album. Just have the subjects lean in close together and click. (CAMERA: Nikon D2X, ISO: 800, LIGHTING: on-camera flash)

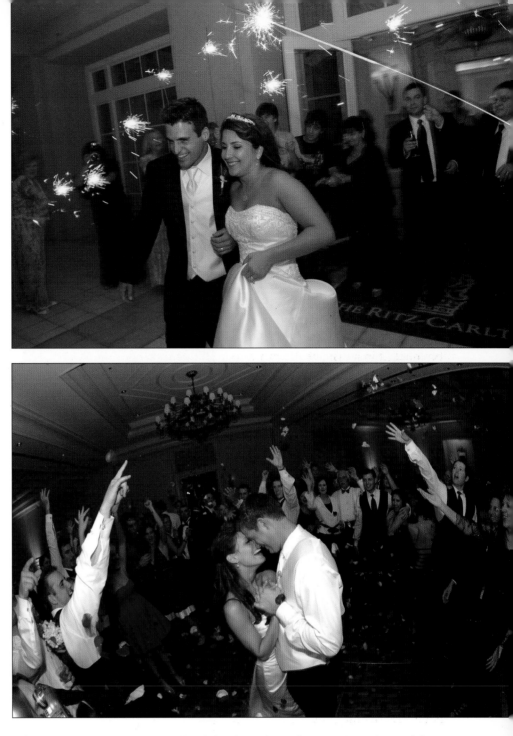

Top—Guests waved sparkers to mark this couple's exit from the reception. (CAMERA: Nikon D2X, ISO: 800, LENS: 17–55mm at 17mm, EXPOSURE: 1/40 second at f/4, LIGHTING: on-camera flash)

Bottom—At some weddings, the couple enjoys a dance at the end of the reception while guests throw rose petals. (CAMERA: Nikon D2Xs, ISO: 800, LENS: 10.5mm fisheye, EXPOSURE: 1/60 second at f/4.5, LIGHTING: on-camera flash)

nouncements (such as guest birthdays), and Uncle Lou out of control on the dance floor. Be ready. Be aware.

EXIT SHOTS

As the night winds down, the reception will usually conclude with some type of exit or other official ending. It may be as simple as a last dance with flower petals tossed, or it could be a sparkler exit. Who knows—it might even be a helicopter picking the couple up. Whatever it is, be ready and position yourself to capture it.

CHECK YOUR GEAR

Now that the night is over, do a quick inventory of your gear. Make sure you have everything. Remember: have a place for everything and put everything in its place. We have a memory card wallet and we confirm that all of our cards are accounted for and in the wallet. You can insure your gear against loss or theft, but if you misplace your cards, you have trouble. If anything is amiss, deal with it right away. It is a lot easier to retrace your steps then and there than to return the next day after everything has been cleaned and moved.

SECURE YOUR IMAGES

At the conclusion of the event, it is critical to secure your images. We tend to download our images that night because we enjoy seeing what we have captured. However, it is okay to wait until the next morning. What's essential is that you have an established process.

We download all of the cards onto our Macintosh computer's hard drive. All of our cameras are synced to the right time, making it easy to organize the files chronologically. We then use a program called Photo Mechanic to edit and rename our files (you could also use Adobe Lightroom or ACDSee). As we download each card, we rename it and then bring in another card. Once everything is downloaded and renamed we burn a backup DVD or DVDs. These are labeled as originals and stored in a CD/DVD binder in a location other than our studio. These are emergency backups of the original files that we can always go back to—even in the event of a fire or other catastrophe at the studio. We also back up to DVD our polished and edited versions of the files, which are kept in a binder at the studio.

WE TEND TO DOWNLOAD OUR IMAGES THAT NIGHT BECAUSE WE ENJOY SEEING WHAT WE HAVE CAPTURED.

This gives us backups in triplicate in multiple locations. It's a pretty rudimentary system, but it has worked effectively so far—knock on wood. We are also looking to get a NASD (Network Attached Storage Device) at our studio where all the data will live and it will have automatic backup and RAID capabilities. We will still implement the previous system before the data goes there, however; you can never have too many backups.

9. Seven Time-Saving Strategies

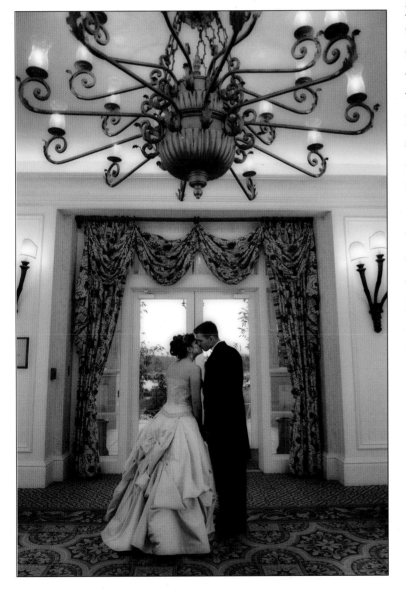

Missed a moment? If appropriate, try to make up it. For example, if you missed this shot, it would be simple to ask them to kiss one more time. (**CAMERA:** Nikon D2X, **ISO:** 800, **LENS:** 17–55mm at 17mm, **EXPOSURE:** ¹⁄₂₀ second at f/2.8, **OTHER:** tripod)

HEN I WAS A YOUNG PHOTOGRAPHER AT WALT DISNEY WORLD, I was sent out to photograph a group shot of three hundred people for the United Way. This was considered a one-man job, so I set out armed with my Hasselblad and two Photogenic power lights. On these jobs you typically had some time beforehand to choose where you would shoot and do a Polaroid. When it was time to execute the photograph, however, you would only have about ten minutes—and often less. That is about how long it takes for a group of three-hundred people to get bored and start heading for the cocktail area.

To get the shot, I had to climb into a lighting tech booth overlooking a dance floor that would accommodate everyone. By looking down at the clients, I could effectively pose everyone and place the key players in a prominent position. I got there early, made friends with the lighting guys, set up my lights, and did a Polaroid. I was ready to rock-n-roll—at least that's what I thought.

The clients came in and I executed the shot, then crawled down the catwalk. However, when I went to roll out the film, nausea ensued. You see, Hasselblads are excellent cameras. I really love them. However, there is one thing about them: when you load the film you need to wind the crank to frame number one or you are just shooting on paper. In fact, there are usually about six frames on paper before you get to the film—the exact number I had just shot. I had just shot the group on paper. This wasn't good, and I was sick to my stomach.

I explained the situation to my liaison, however, and he quickly told the client that some bigwigs had arrived late and we need to do the shot again. Everybody grumbled, but they reluctantly agreed—and a bullet was dodged.

The point to this story is that you can almost always make something up if you need to—especially at a wedding. The key is that you have to recognize your mistakes or successes instantaneously and not be frivolous with your time. You never know when you might need an extra ten minutes to reshoot something. Time is your enemy, because it is the one thing that you will never be able to control.

This leads us to our seven strategies for combating Father Time. They are:

1. Be an opportunist.
2. Listen.
3. Use available light.
4. See beyond what is there.
5. Recognize success or failure instantly.
6. Train your anticipatory and reactive skills.
7. Become one with your assistant.

Be an Opportunist

How many times do we arrive to find that the bride is not ready? Instead of waiting there for an hour, shoot. There is always something to capture. You need to train yourself to be an opportunist. Look closely for anything that will help tell the story of her day. Details make excellent transitions in the album and are effective emotional reminders to the bride and groom of their special day. Capture the bridal bouquet lying on a table, a note from the groom, a card from a friend, the bride's shoes, her necklace, the dress, her grandmother's brooch. After you make these shots, walk around and get some establishing shots. Never rest and never waste any of that time.

THERE IS ALWAYS SOMETHING TO CAPTURE. YOU NEED TO TRAIN YOURSELF TO BE AN OPPORTUNIST.

Photojournalists who visit the Amazon or cover wars sometimes live with the indigenous people for two weeks before they even pull out their camera.

There is always something to capture—like this image of the bride's custom-made, one-of-a-kind ring box. (CAMERA: Nikon D2Xs, ISO: 500, LENS: 70–200mm at 70mm, EXPOSURE: $\frac{1}{160}$ second at f/2.8)

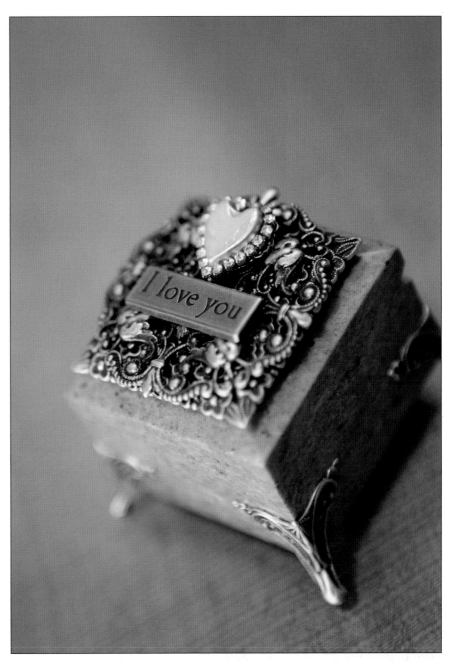

That way, the people are comfortable with them; they break the shield of self consciousness so they can get to the soul of their subjects. You do not have that luxury. What you do have, however, is the possibility of an engagement session before the wedding. Engagement sessions provide more than just lovely pictures that can be displayed at the wedding, they establish a level of trust between you and your clients. If done properly, the bride and groom will be a lot less self conscious. It is hardly a two-week acclamation period, but it helps immensely.

At the wedding, you must be like a hunter stalking his prey. This sounds a little dramatic, but it is true. You must use all of your senses to pick up on the little nuances that are happening around you. The wedding ritual is abundant with opportunities. Train your self to see, hear, and feel them. This way you will always come away with above-average results—whatever the wedding throws at you. You will also begin to develop your own unique way of looking at things. This is the beginning of developing your own visual style.

Real moments are priceless. Always be on the lookout for them. A mother's tear, a smile from a friend, or the father's first meeting with his daughter in her dress. Don't, however, relax in between them. We think it is perfectly acceptable to make things happen, if necessary. You do not need to be obtrusive; on the contrary, you must be as unobtrusive as possible, but how hard is it to say, "Hey—can you hug her again?" or "Do you mind lacing up her dress by this window?" With suggestions like these, you can subtly take charge of the situation. You have finite time parameters and only you know what you have in the can. So step up and use your time wisely.

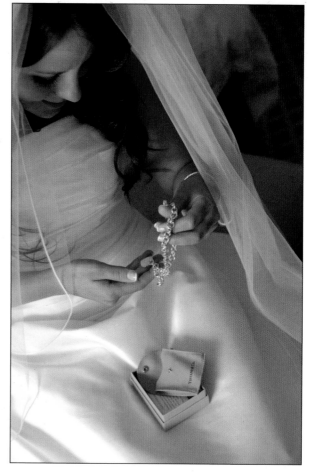

LISTEN

I have mentioned the need to use all of your senses. Your ears, in particular, are a very valuable commodity at a wedding. When you first arrive at the wedding, listen. Introduce yourself and your associate, but after that try to be a fly on the wall. Eavesdrop on some of the hot issues of the day. Find out who is getting or not getting along with whom. This will help you know who not to pose by whom. If you train yourself to listen effectively you'll usually know everything you need to know about their family by the time the ceremony starts.

We love to call people by their names; it invokes an instant bond and people are more likely to listen when you address them by name, making your job a little easier. Sometimes, however, we forget a name. It may be necessary to simply ask the name again, but if you just listen, chances are the other folks in the room will call that person by his/her name eventually. Just by tuning in, you will be the hero who remembers everything about your clients.

Above—Real moments are priceless. Here, the bride opens a Tiffany bracelet from the groom. This is not a good time to take a break—you have to remain alert and ready to capture every moment. (CAMERA: Nikon D2Xs, ISO: 500, LENS: 17–55mm at 44mm, EXPOSURE: $\frac{1}{100}$ second at f/4)

Facing page—This image captured the bride's nervous last moment before she entered the church. The portrait was beautifully lit by available light—late-day sun through a window. (CAMERA: Nikon D2Xs, ISO: 320, LENS: 50mm f/1.4, EXPOSURE: $\frac{1}{160}$ second at f/4)

USE AVAILABLE LIGHT

The best advice I could give a new photographer is to turn off your flash. Start shooting without one and you will experience much more natural results. It requires good technique, but if executed properly the results can be

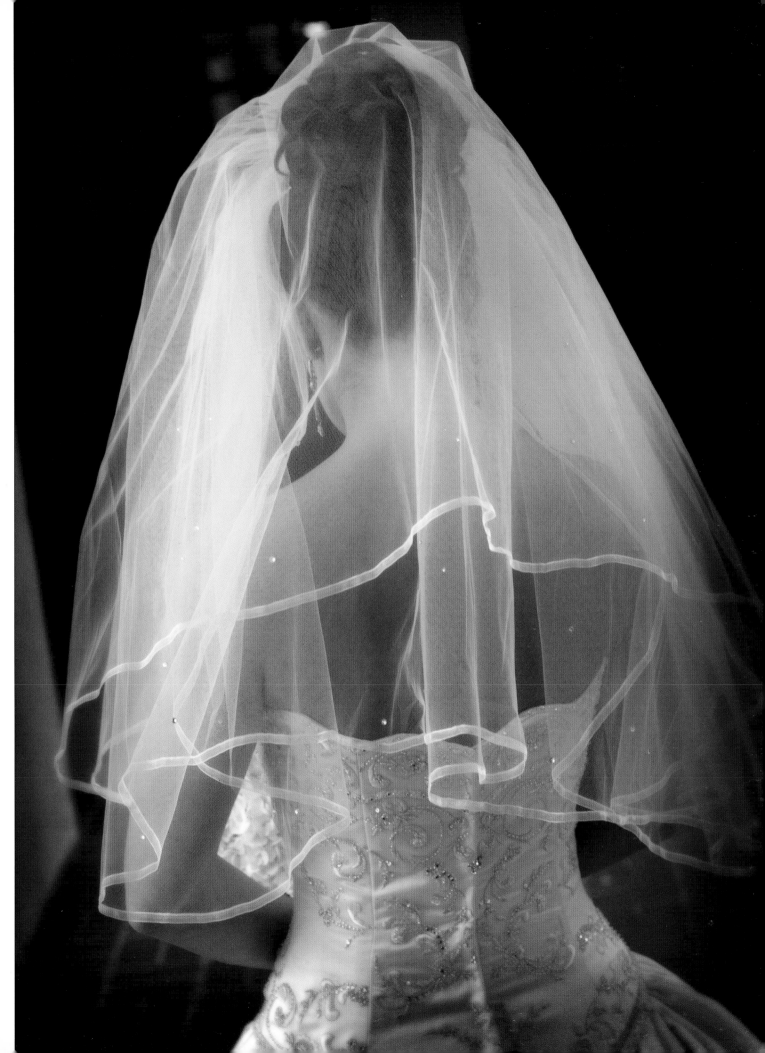

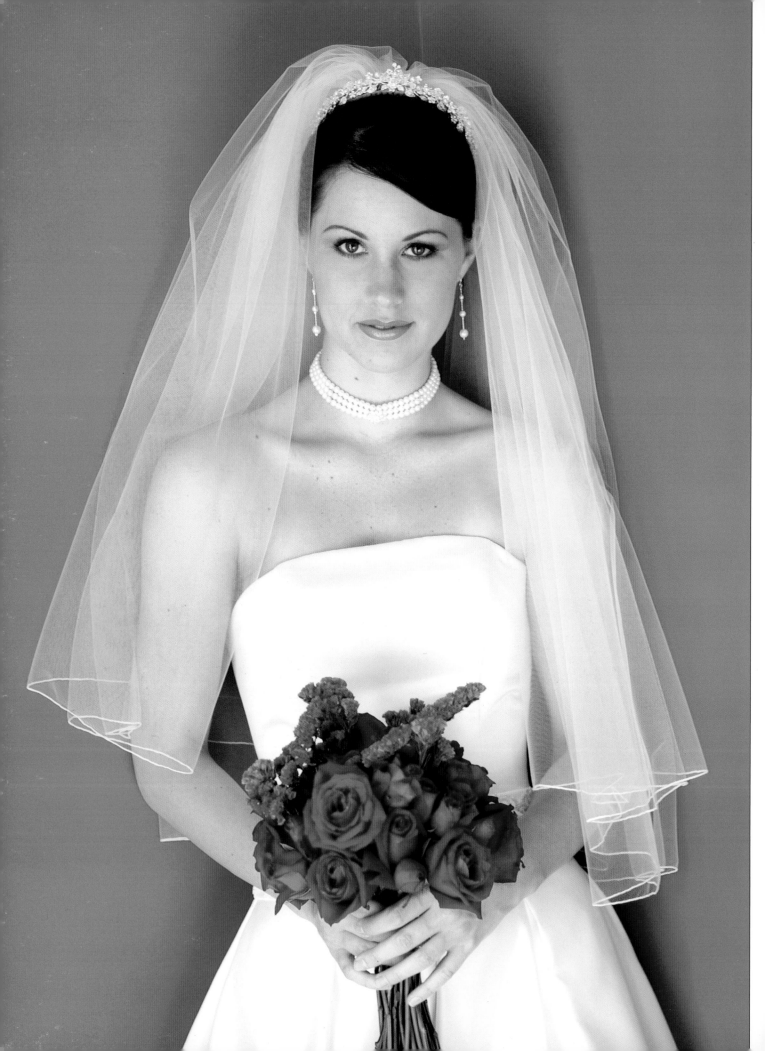

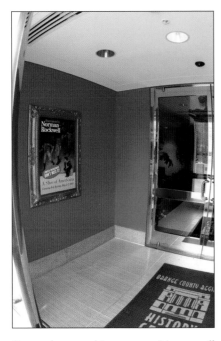

Great photographic opportunities are all around you. This location (above) might not have looked like much at first glance, but there was great window light and a vibrant red wall. The result is a memorable portrait (facing page). (**CAMERA:** Nikon D1X, **ISO:** 400, **LENS:** 50mm f/1.4, **EXPOSURE:** 1/25 second at f/2.8)

much more dramatic photographs. With available light, there's nothing to carry and no extra equipment to slow you down. The key to using natural light successfully is training your eye to see it. This is a topic we have looked at throughout this book, and it will be covered in greater detail in chapter 11.

SEE BEYOND WHAT IS THERE

"From there to here, from here to there, funny things are everywhere." That is what Dr. Seuss thought about funny things. I see photographic opportunities the same way as he sees humor. They are all around us. We mindlessly walk by them all day long.

At Disney, I was trained early on by some wonderful photographers. One in particular was Michael Glen Taylor, who revolutionized the way I looked at everything. Michael taught me to work around the light—to find great lighting and then look for the background. Michael would walk around with a model and say, "Stop, that is it!" His students often could not see it until he pulled a Polaroid—and then we were all blown away. He would show us slideshows of beautiful portraits and we would think he had shot them in an incredible botanical garden. The next slide, however, would reveal that the portraits were actually taken in a not-so-nice city park with trash cans and homeless people just outside of his compositions.

The point is this: training yourself with this type of mindful visualization empowers you to pull wonderful images out of your hat, no matter the sit-

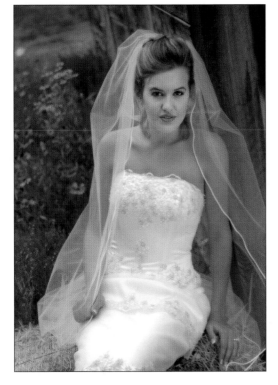

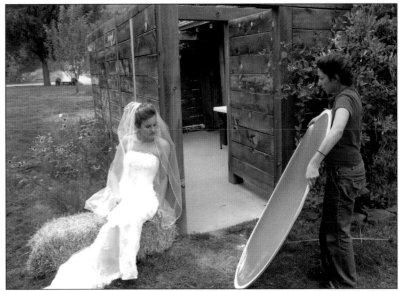

This image (left) was shot at an outdoor wedding in Colorado. The location (above) for this photograph would have been easy to walk right by. With the addition of a silver reflector, a high camera angle, and a shallow depth of field it was perfect for a rustic bridal portrait. (**CAMERA:** Nikon D2X, **ISO:** 200, **LENS:** 17–55mm at 55mm, **EXPOSURE:** 1/800 second at f/2.8)

uation. Whether it is raining, snowing, full sun, cloudy, or a level-four hurricane, you have options.

I was once commissioned to take some photos for a wedding magazine at an old courthouse in downtown Orlando. Upon entering the courthouse, I noticed the vibrant red corner that was lit perfectly by natural light from a window (see page 90–91). I placed the model in the corner and had an assistant hold a reflector to pop a little light into the model's eyes. In about four minutes we had the shot (and it would have taken only two minutes, but the automatic door kept closing on me, so we had to be patient!). How many of you would have just walked on by?

RECOGNIZE SUCCESS OR FAILURE INSTANTLY

Digital is a wonderful tool. The instant feedback provided by the LCD and histogram is one of the best tools at your disposal for ensuring more professional results. You can quickly zoom in to check your focus, see if the eyes are open, and verify your exposure in seconds. (Just think about all the money and trouble we used to go through to shoot Polaroids!)

With digital, you know when you have the shot and you can move on. This enables you to try things outside of your comfort zone. If you are too far off the mark, your LCD/histogram will tell you and you can instantly make corrections or abort the effort. This saves valuable time, which is imperative for today's weddings. Brides want to enjoy their day and they will not endure a three-hour photo session. They want to have fun—and if you want to stay competitive, you will let them.

TRAIN YOUR ANTICIPATORY AND REACTIVE SKILLS

The sixth strategy to combat time is anticipatory and reactive training. The wedding ritual is rich with events that happen time and time again. As a professional, you need to be in the right place at the right time and ready to capture some real emotions.

The first moments typically happen as the bride is getting ready—a mother's glance, a nervous bride, the bridesmaids laughing. Be ready and position yourself accordingly. The ceremony is also ripe with opportunity. We always shoot their reactions when the bride and groom first see each other. Couples really love these shots, because they are usually so entranced by the moment that they hardly remember it.

Next, the minister will usually say, "Who gives this women to this man?" Typically the dad will say, "We do," and give his daughter a kiss on the cheek, then shake the groom's hand. Boo-ya! Another moment captured, because

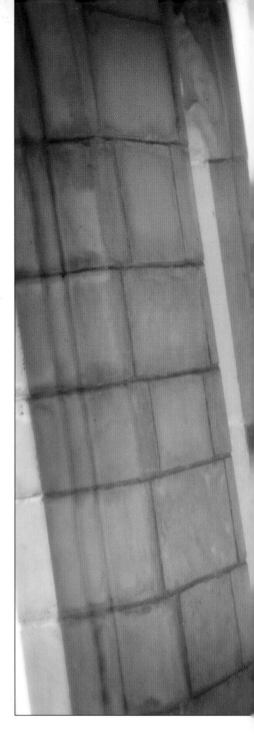

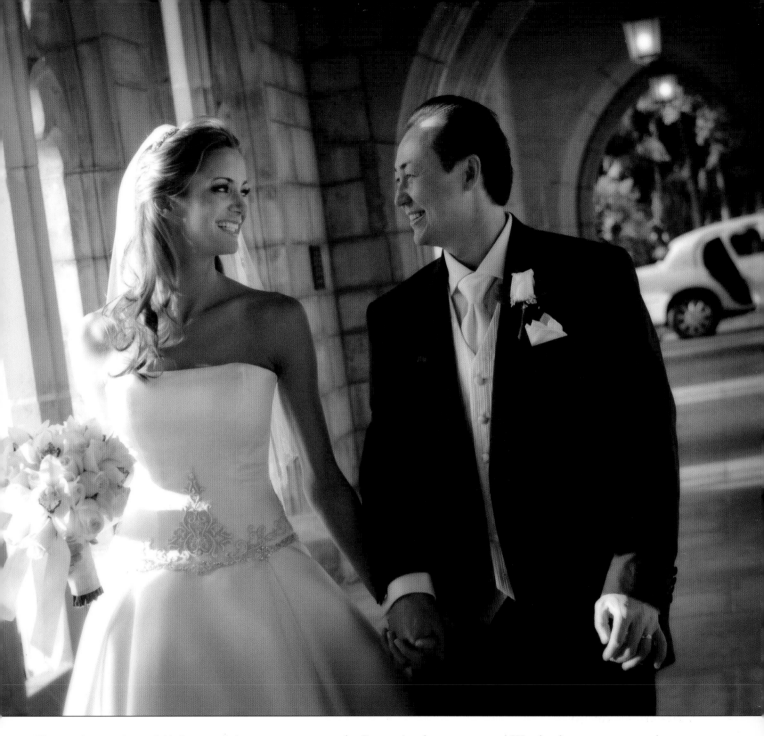

The genuine emotions of this just-married couple are evident on their faces. (CAMERA: Nikon D2X, ISO: 400, LENS: 17–55mm at 55mm, EXPOSURE: ¹⁄₁₆₀ second at f/4.5)

you were ready. But wait, there are more. We also love to capture close-up reactions of the guests. At the usual spots (vows, ring exchange, kiss) you can usually get some excellent expressions.

Immediately after the ceremony, if you follow the bride and groom you may be rewarded with some truly giddy, love-struck expressions. The bride and groom will still be totally wrapped up in the moment and probably won't even realize you are there, documenting every moment. After the ceremony, people will congratulate the bride and groom. These can be very nice images as well.

At the reception, the first dance and parent dances have some priceless expressions. Following the toasts you can also expect to see some photogenic hugs. Be ready.

There are wonderful, memorable moments at every wedding; these are just some of the many expected ones. The point is: be ready! Don't just react. Anticipate, then execute. You might not be right all the time, but when you are, you will have positioned yourself for success. Wedding photography is a thinking person's sport. By anticipating the action and nailing the shot, you can save yourself the time and headache of having to "restage" something—and probably come away with some real emotions in your photos.

> YOU MIGHT NOT BE RIGHT ALL THE TIME, BUT WHEN YOU ARE, YOU WILL HAVE POSITIONED YOURSELF FOR SUCCESS.

BE ONE WITH YOUR ASSISTANT

Being one with your assistant is a valuable time saver. How many times have you looked up and seen them in your viewfinder? Curses, foiled again.

Good associates are hard to come by. If you find a responsible one with a good eye, nurture them. After each wedding, review your shots together. Identify what worked and what did not. Grow together. If you want them to

There are many memorable moments at every wedding. Careful planning will allow you to capture them all. (CAMERA: Nikon D2X, ISO: 800, LENS: 70–200mm at 86mm, EXPOSURE: 1/50 second at f/2.8)

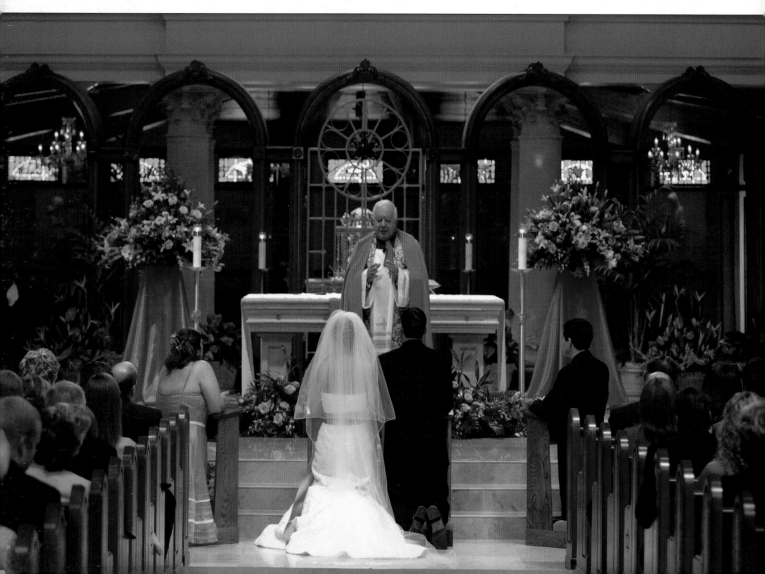

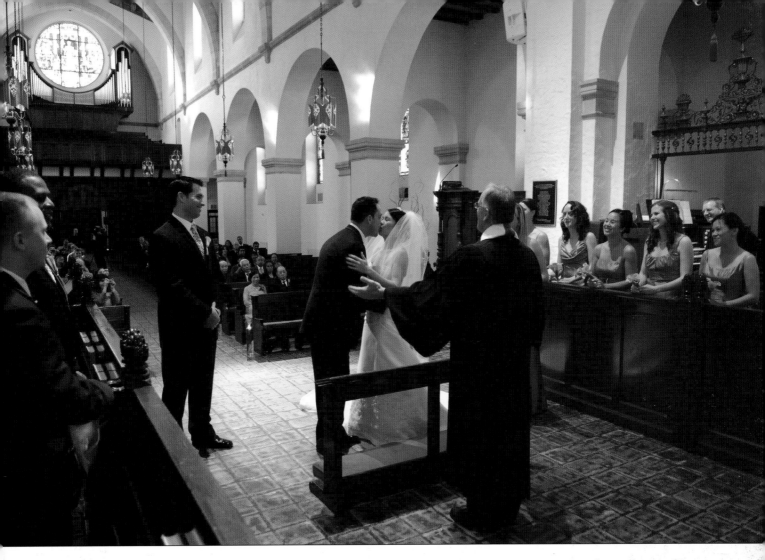

The second shooter was able to capture a unique perspective on this kiss shot. (CAMERA: Nikon D2X, ISO: 800, LENS: 17–55mm at 17mm, EXPOSURE: ¹⁄₄₀ second at f/2.8, OTHER: tripod)

be as focused on the wedding as you are, you must give them plenty of incentives (encouragement, money, support) to do well. Give them some freedom, as well. In my early days, I wanted my associates to shoot and be just like me. Now that I am a little older and wiser, I let them be themselves and am amazed at some of the results. Work toward a more symbiotic relationship where both parties gain value from the experience.

All in all, there must be good communication. Hand signals can be really helpful, since screaming across the church during the ceremony is not a good idea. Basically, you just want a plan of action, so you are not both shooting the same exact shot. Once you have a good assistant, you'll find they are an invaluable timesaver. How else can you be two places at once?

Like death and taxes, the passing of time is inevitable, so don't waste it. These seven strategies should help you maximize your productivity at the wedding. They are tried-and-true techniques for being successful as a wedding photographer.

10. Posing Techniques

*L*ET'S FACE IT: IT IS EASY TO CREATE A LIKENESS OF A PERSON. To make a portrait that they truly love . . . now that's a different story. Our subjects come to us to document them in some stage of their life. They also hope, at the very least, that it will be a reasonably flattering manner. There are a few simple techniques that our studio employs to achieve this.

CAMERA ANGLE

The camera typically adds a few pounds, something most clients won't appreciate. To compensate for this, we tend to use a higher camera angle on our portraits. Try this experiment. Ask a friend or family member to sit on a chair. Then, while you are standing above them, look down at their face. Next, switch places and look up at their face. Which view is more visually appealing? Chances are when you were looking down at them they looked much better. Upward angles may be great for supermodels, but for the normal person it exacerbates any facial flaws and makes that double chin a quadruple chin.

Where you position your camera, what lens you use, and how you light your subject all have profound effect on the outcome of your photograph. Typically, we try to maximize the positive and minimize any flaws. I know this all too well because,

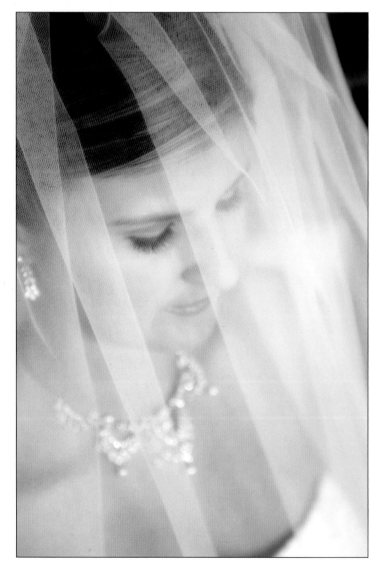

For most people, a high camera angle is very flattering. Here, the drama was increased by shooting through the bride's blusher veil. (**CAMERA:** Nikon, **ISO:** 400, **LENS:** 17–55mm at 55mm, **EXPOSURE:** $^1/_{100}$ second at f/2.8, **LIGHTING:** available)

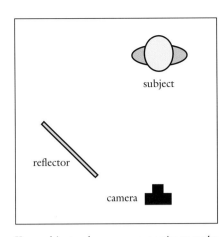

Your subjects rely on your expertise to make them look their very best, so use every tool in your arsenal to ensure they truly love their images. (**CAMERA:** Nikon D70, **ISO:** 200, **LENS:** 10.5mm fisheye, **EXPOSURE:** $^1/_{500}$ second at f/5.0)

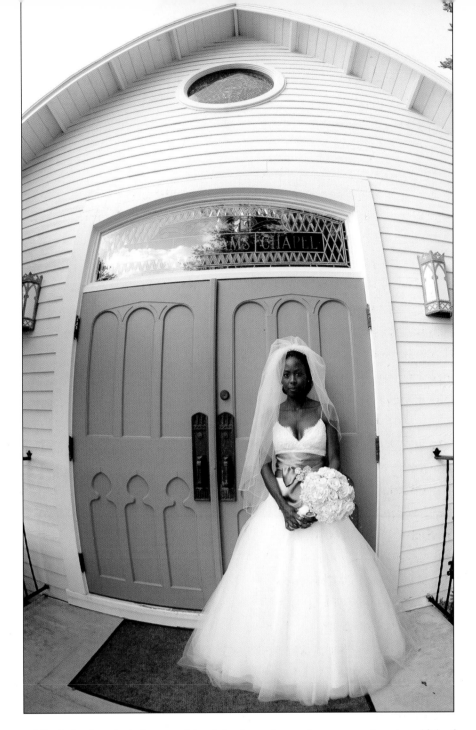

while I don't mind the way I look in the mirror, there are only a handful of shots of myself that I really love—and many of them I set up myself. The reason is exactly what we have been discussing: most snapshots are done from a low angle with a wide-angle lens. If you have a big head like mine, it is going to be *really* big when photographed that way! So our studio is extremely sensitive about using all of our tools to make someone look their best.

Let's say, for instance, we have a full-figured bride who has a beautiful face. To photographer her, we'll use a high angle and do a close-up headshot that crops out most of her body, and she'll love us for it. If we have a groom with an unusually large nose, we'll avoid doing many profile photos with him. Its sound like pretty basic common sense, and it is—but you would be surprised how many photographers don't employ these tricks.

POSING BASICS

Not all of our wedding clients are models. Typically, they do not have an arsenal of poses in their repertoire. Sure, they may giggle if you ask them for Ben Stiller's Magnum or Blue Steel pose (from the movie *Zoolander*), but that is about it. They usually need a little direction.

We are all about real moments, but we also want to capture some stylish fashion images, so we are not embarrassed to say we are posers. Early in my career, Disney sent me to study with Monte Zucker and Clay Blackmore. I would drive to Sarasota once a month and attend classes and spent a substantial amount of time learning how to get the bride's wrists to look just right. This, although beautiful, seemed a little excessive in the world that the great Tony Corbell coined "Guerrilla Wedding Photography." There was, however, a lot of good that came out of these classes. I learned to put people together quickly and with good aesthetic results. I also learned how subtle refinements make huge differences and that hands and feet are crucial to a good portrait. I used the knowledge gained from these sessions to develop my own style: stylized fashion/documentary.

POSING THE GROOM

When photographing grooms, we like to lean the subject up against a wall, cross his ankles, and put his hands in his trouser pockets. This pose has a contemporary look to it, and having him lean on something tends to relax him. We tell him to act like he's waiting for a bus.

This is our normal male pose. Typically, it would not be presented as a full-length image, but the entire subject is shown here to illustrate how crossing the ankles puts the rest of the body into the correct position. (CAMERA: Nikon D2Xs, ISO: 400, LENS: 17–55mm at f/4, EXPOSURE: $\frac{1}{100}$ second at f/4)

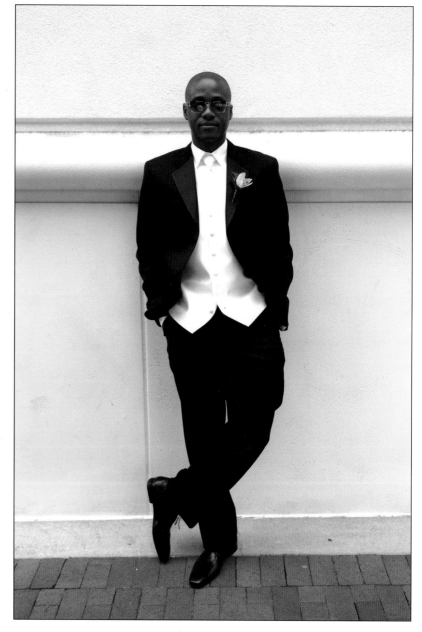

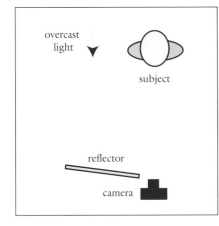

Using a banister helps get the groom into a perfect masculine pose. (**CAMERA:** Nikon D2X, **ISO:** 160, **LENS:** 17–55mm f/2.8 at 52mm, **EXPOSURE:** $1/160$ second at f/2.8)

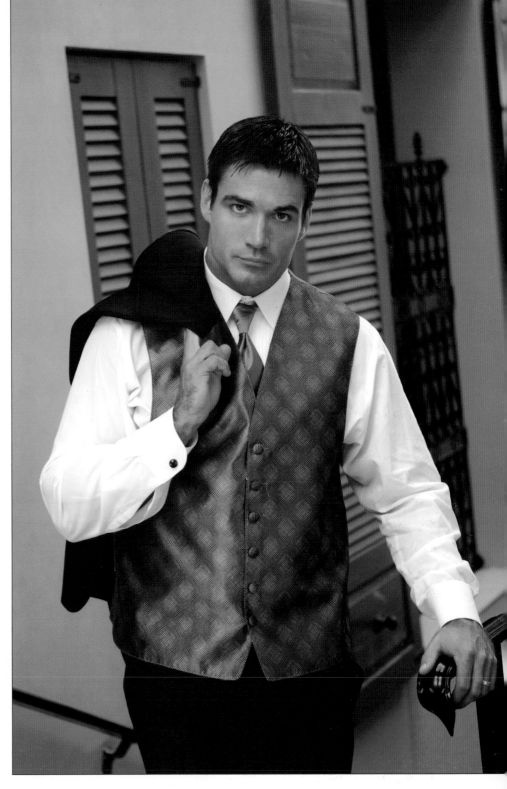

The positioning of the feet and hands is critical to this portrait. Having the groom cross his ankles puts his body in the perfect masculine pose. This provides the foundation for your portrait. Whether to place the hands in or out of the pockets has been debated forever, so do what looks good to you. Remember, however, that by putting them in the pockets, you get rid of a potentially distracting item (i.e., spread-out or awkward-looking finger situations). An otherwise wonderful portrait can be ruined if your subject does something strange with his fingers and ends up looking like he only has two digits on his right hand. Yes, hands can make or break a great photograph. We are working against the clock, so we usually just have grooms stick their hands in their trouser pockets. Another technique is to have them close their hands loosely as if they had a golf pencil clasped inside. You could even have one hand in the pocket and the other at the side.

Normally, we will show them the pose. This is very important. Actually leaning up against the wall and doing the pose is a huge time saver. If you show them what you want them to do, they get it instantly. From there, we kind of let it happen. If they deviate a little from it, but it still looks aesthetically pleasing, that's fine. The hard-and-fast rule of days gone by are *gone*. The hand police have all retired. We are just trying to make a nice-looking portrait in a timely way.

Another pose we like to use for the groom is where he is leaning on a rail or chair. Again, the groom's feet and hands must be refined. Even if his feet are not in the photograph, it is important to cross them because it naturally places his upper body in the correct position. Typically, you want to light the short side of the face. This provides a slimming effect.

POSING THE BRIDE

The pose we use most often for the bride harkens back to a famous sculpture, the Venus de Milo. This pose

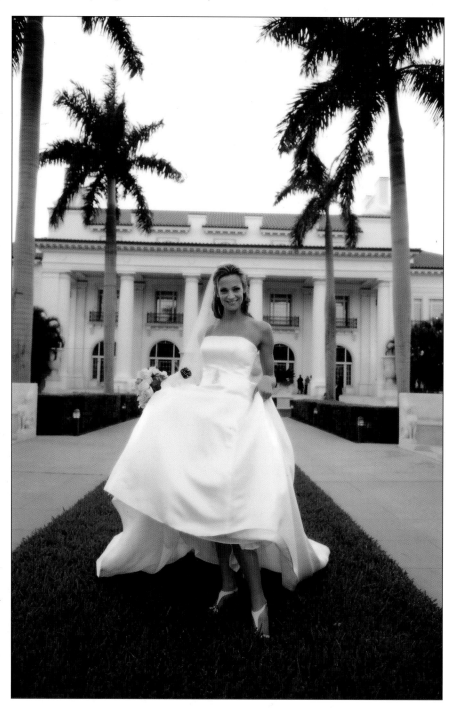

This elegant shot of the bride was taken in all of two minutes while we were late for the reception. Note the position of her feet. (CAMERA: Nikon D2Xs, ISO: 640, LENS: 17–55mm at 17mm, EXPOSURE: ¹/₁₀₀ second at f/2.8)

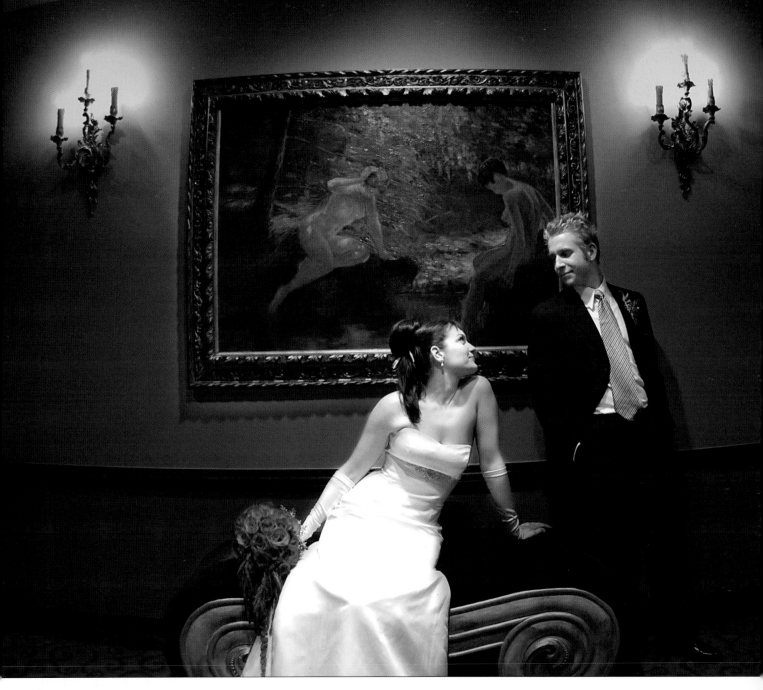

Shot with existing can lights (a row of small, ceiling-mounted lights above the couple), this portrait shows a good seated pose for the bride. (**CAMERA:** Nikon D1X, **ISO:** 800, **LENS:** 16mm, **EXPOSURE:** ¹⁄₄₀ second at f/2.8, **OTHER:** tripod)

starts with the bride's feet in an L position. This pose will work with either the right foot forward or the left forward, whichever features your subject best. In this example, we'll assume her right foot is forward. With her weight slightly on her back foot, her shoulders and torso will normally turn to the right. We will then bring her chin back to the left, her flowers to one side, and her free hand to the other side. As with the guys, watch for splayed or awkward finger arrangements; these will ruin your image. This is the feminine pose. It is a tried and true form that you would do well to learn. As with the masculine pose, we illustrate this pose to the bride. It is usually good for a laugh.

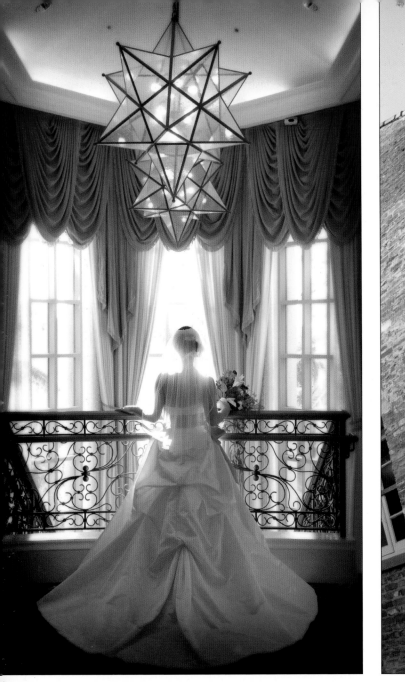

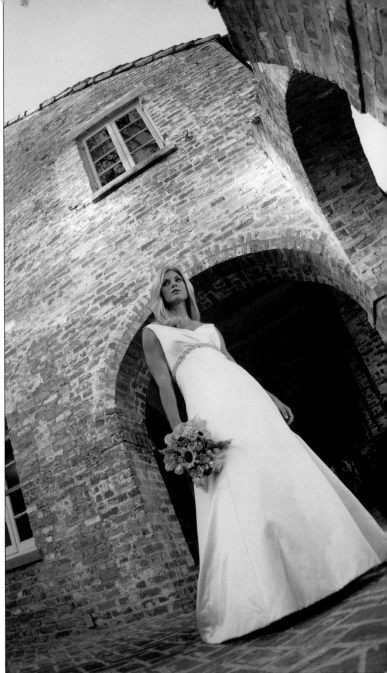

A modern variation of this pose is to have the bride lean on a wall and cross her ankles. If she is not heavy, you can shoot her more square-on for a contemporary fashion look. Another variation of this pose is the seated bridal portrait. Chaises longues are great for this shot in which the seated bride sweeps her crossed ankles to one side, leans forward, and brings her chin to the side of her body opposite her feet.

Another pose that we employ with the bride is a shot from behind that showcases the dress. Typically we like to do this in front of a window. Once again, the bride's feet are in the L position with her back square to us. You can break this rule and just have her look out the window naturally. Both approaches are effective.

Left—With the bride's feet in an L position, she was photographed from the back to showcase her dress. (CAMERA: Nikon D2Xs, ISO: 400, LENS: 17–55mm at 26mm, EXPOSURE: 1/60 second at f/4)

Right—An extreme upward angle and fashion pose will work for modelesque brides. (CAMERA: Nikon D1X, ISO: 400, LENS: 16mm, EXPOSURE: 1/400 second at f/2.8)

Lastly, if your clients do happen to look like supermodels you can shoot up from an extremely low angle with a fashion pose. This creates a very dynamic image, but it is not for your overweight clients.

POSING THE BRIDE AND GROOM TOGETHER

The next challenge is photographing the bride and groom together. This is essentially a combination of the two previous poses, but there is a little variation with the groom. To simplify this, we will begin by putting both the bride and groom in L poses. *(Note:* The groom is typically on the right because he has a boutonniere on his left lapel. There are no rules, however. If the bride looks better on the other side, put her there. If the boutonniere bothers you, take it off.)

Then, have them place their inside arms around each other's backs. Again, hand placement is critical. Be careful not to let their hands go around each other too far, and don't let them place their hands on each other's shoulders. Models can pull this off, but with the bride and groom, these misplaced hands can look like strange growths emanating from their bodies. The safe bet is for the groom to put his hand on the bride's rear and for the bride to put her inside hand on the small of the groom's back.

To finish the pose, the groom simply puts his outside hand in his pocket and the bride places her flowers down low on her outside hip. Voilà!

In the basic L position, the couple lean in for a kiss as confetti canons go off around them. (**CAMERA:** Nikon D70s, **ISO:** 100, **LENS:** 10.5mm fisheye, **EXPOSURE:** ¹⁄₁₀₀ second at f/3.2)7

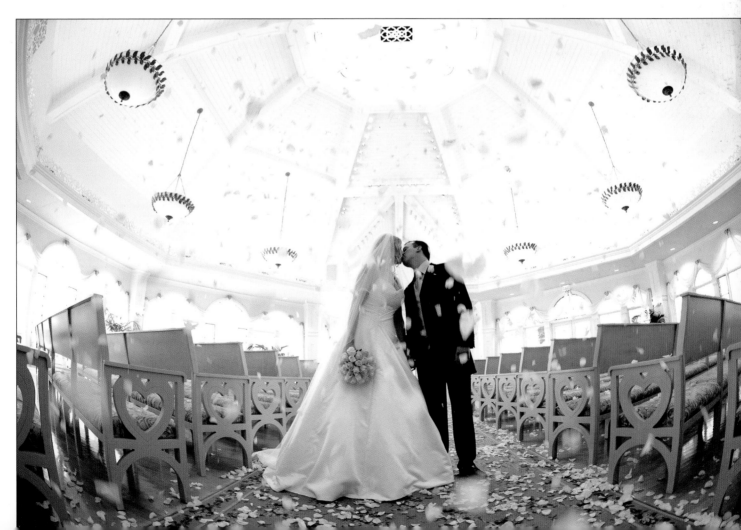

From here you can do a number of variations. For one shot, ask the bride and groom to look at each other while not moving their bodies, just their heads. That's one shot. Then have them lean in and kiss. That's another shot. We also like to have the brides and grooms lean on walls. We might even have the groom lean on a lamppost and the bride lean in. These are all variations of the L pose.

Another thing to be mindful of when posing brides and grooms is how they fit together. What we mean by this is that usually their heads or bodies are not the same size. There are ways to approach this methodically that will yield above-average results. For instance, whatever you put closest to the lens generally appears larger than something farther from the lens. This is exacerbated with wide-angle photography. Let's say that you have a groom with a smaller head than the bride. If you place her closes to the camera than him, it will further accentuate this discrepancy. If, however, you simply switch

Left—Archways can provide dramatic framing elements. This is a variation of the L pose. (**CAMERA**: Nikon D2X, **ISO**: 160, **LENS**: 50mm f/1.4, **EXPOSURE**: $\frac{1}{125}$ second at f/6.3)

Right—This groom had a very narrow face, but by placing him slightly closer to the camera than the bride, their faces appear well matched. (**CAMERA**: Nikon D2X, **ISO**: 250, **LENS**: 17–55mm at 52mm, **EXPOSURE**: $\frac{1}{500}$ second at f/2.8)

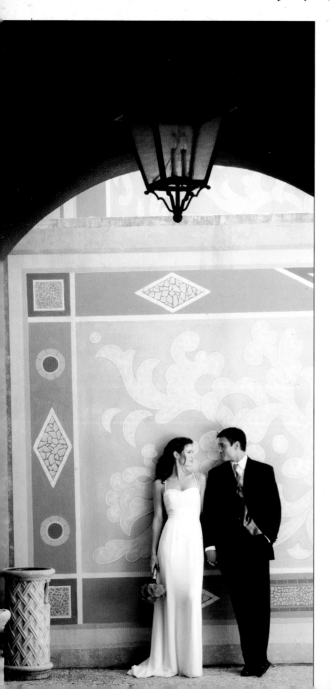

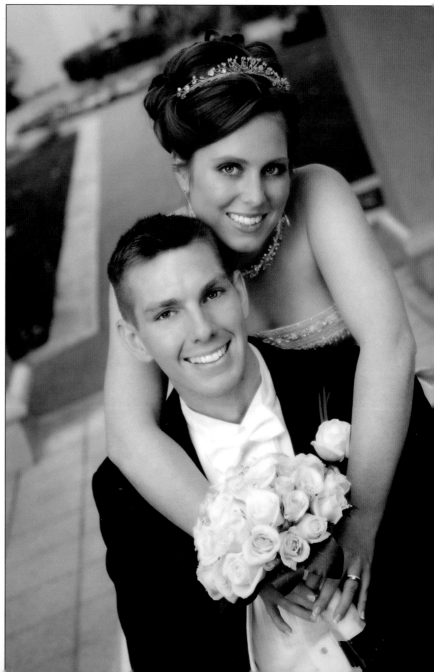

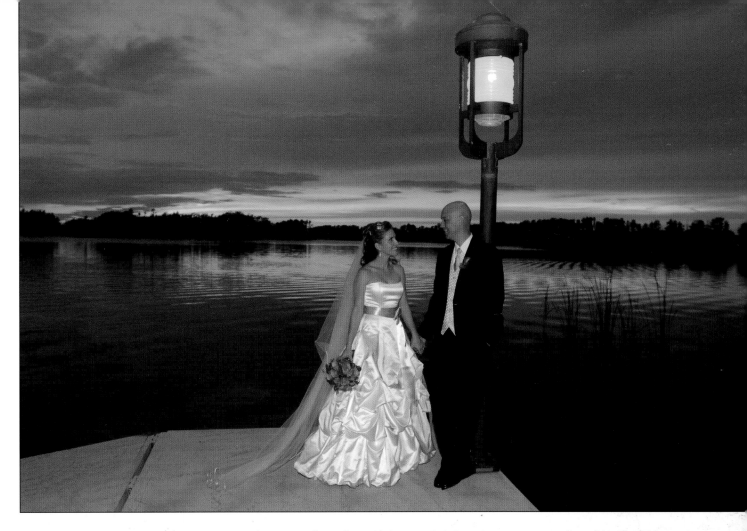

Another variation of the basic L pose has the groom leaning back and the couple holding hands. (**CAMERA:** Nikon D2Xs, **ISO:** 800, **LENS:** 17– 35mm at 17mm, **EXPOSURE:** ¹/₄₀ second at f/3.5, **OTHER:** tripod)

them, it will work much better. It is just common sense, but this mindfulness of people's features will serve you well.

Similarly, in the side-by-side L pose, if you want to diminish the size of your subject relative to their partner, have them positioned an inch or so back. This technique does not work all that well with telephoto lenses, but with wide-angle and medium lenses it can make a dramatic difference. Remember, we are trying to make these people look good.

POSING THE FAMILIES

The side-by-side L pose is also the building block for all the family portrait and group shots—just keep the bride and groom in place for each shot and position other subjects around them. Be sure to tell the bride and groom that they should hold their positions, as you are under time constraints. It just wastes time if the bride or groom goes off and starts chatting with someone. It is better if they just hold their pose and you keep building on it.

We start with the parents. With the groom's hand in his pocket, we have the mother grab the groom's outside arm as if he were escorting her down the aisle. The father steps under the dress (typically these shots are waist up), then puts his hand on the small of the bride's back, carefully making sure to go under the veil and not to pull on it. The veil has some nasty plastic spikes to keep it in place and it can really hurt the bride if someone pulls on it. There it is—the parents' shot is done.

After the parents, we usually do the immediate family. Typically, this includes the mom and dad, any brothers and/or sisters, and the bride and groom. Usually, we will have the mom get next to her son or daughter, then place the dad outside of the mom. The brother and/or sister will be on the opposite side, usually with the sister on the inside and the brother on the outside. The gentlemen on the end will have their outside hands in their pockets. This gives the shot a finished look. They will have their inside hands on the small of the back of the person inside them. This is how we do the family shots quickly and easily.

The next pose you will have to execute is the bridal party shot. It, too, is just a minor variation of what we have been talking about. The bride and groom will remain in the L pose and we will build upon that. For this shot, there may be up to twenty people. For large bridal parties (or any large group shots, for that matter), it is imperative to have steps or levels to help with posing. Otherwise, you just have twenty people lined up like Hands Across America (of course, that might make for an interesting panoramic image). Fortunately, churches usually have at least three or four steps or levels somewhere.

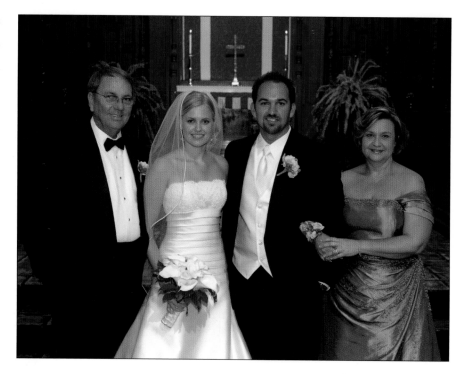

Mom poses next to the groom and Dad poses next to the bride—a typical posing strategy for parent portraits. (CAMERA: Nikon D2X, ISO: 800, LENS: 17–55mm at 32mm, EXPOSURE: 1/50 second at f/4, LIGHTING: on-camera flash, OTHER: tripod)

FLOWER GIRLS AND RING BEARERS ARE TYPICALLY IN THE MIDDLE IN FRONT OF THE BRIDE AND GROOM.

What we do is place the bride or groom on the top level. Then, we place the maid of honor and best man next to the bride and groom. We will then have the bridesmaids sit on the steps in a pose that is similar to the seated bridal pose. Flower girls and ring bearers are typically in the middle in front of the bride and groom.

We then have the groomsmen fill in the rest of the steps. Another technique you can employ is to have two groomsmen take a knee and place a bridesmaid on their upright knees. If your group is too large or you have no steps or levels handy, you can always try to find a high vantage point, such as a balcony or ladder, and shoot down on everyone.

RELAX

There are no hard-and-fast rules on posing anymore. In my opinion, it can be overdone and stifling when executed too precisely. I prefer to offer suggestions and try to let the people be themselves and relax. Our photographers are mindful of the end product and only make refinements when we feel it is in the best interests of our clients. These posing techniques are just tools to help you move more effectively and quickly at your events.

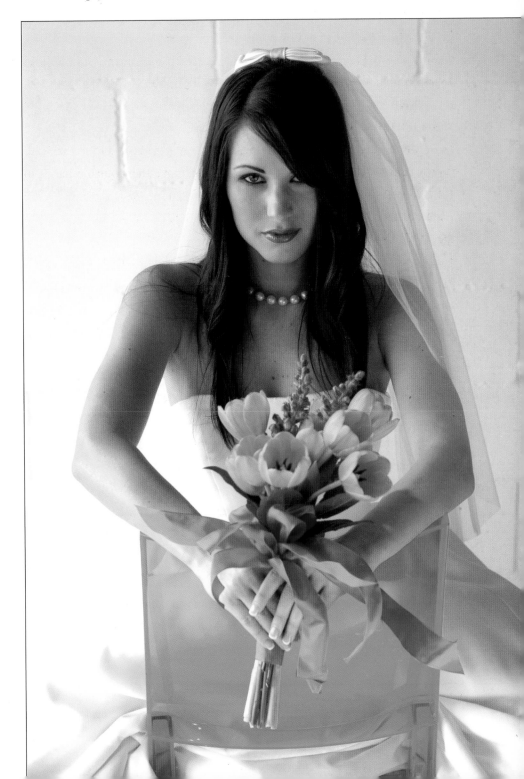

When it comes to posing today's bride, the old "rules" have flown out the window. Let her be herself and use whatever pose makes her look great. (**CAMERA:** Nikon D1X, **ISO:** 400, **LENS:** 50mm f/1.4, **EXPOSURE:** $\frac{1}{80}$ second at f/4)

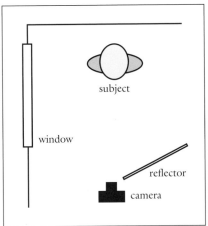

11. Lighting Techniques

WHEN CREATING WEDDING PHOTOGRAPHY, there are three types of light to consider: ambient light (also known as available light), strobe (also known as flash), and continuous light. We use a combination of available light and strobe to achieve our results. We favor available light for wedding photography because of the time constraints that are in place. However, meticulously crafting an image with strobes placed at just the right angles to achieve three-dimensional results on a two dimensional plane is also very rewarding. You can get these three-dimensional results when working with available light, but you will definitely have more control if you have the time (and assistants) to light every portrait with three power lights or Quantum Q-flashes during the wedding. As the wedding photographer, you must constantly make compromises, though. Our studio tries to work as lean and mean as possible. That is our mantra, but you must decide what is right for you and your clients.

WE FAVOR AVAILABLE LIGHT FOR WEDDING PHOTOGRAPHY BECAUSE OF THE TIME CONSTRAINTS THAT ARE IN PLACE.

STROBES

Let's talk about strobes. The upside to using the strobes is a well-lit image at a lower ISO (usually around 400) and a greater f-stop (usually f/8 or f/11). The drawbacks are the need to transport and work with extra gear, and the less natural look that can sometimes result. Don't get us wrong—we love using all of our gadgets and light modifiers, but they just seem to slow us down a little too much in the field.

Strobes are, however, a useful tool and the savvy wedding photographer will have them and know how to employ them. We use the on-camera Nikon SB800 for a lot of our family shots and in all of our candids. If the light is really low, or if we have a lot of time, we will use two Photogenic power lights with umbrellas placed at the ten- and two-o'clock positions. We have a light

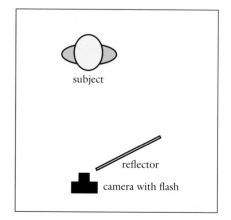

Adding a little fill flash on the bride helped keep the colors in the sky rich and dramatic. (CAMERA: Nikon D2X, ISO: 100, LENS: 17–55mm at 18mm, EXPOSURE: $\frac{1}{250}$ second at f/10, LIGHTING: on-camera flash at $\frac{1}{2}$ stop less than ambient light)

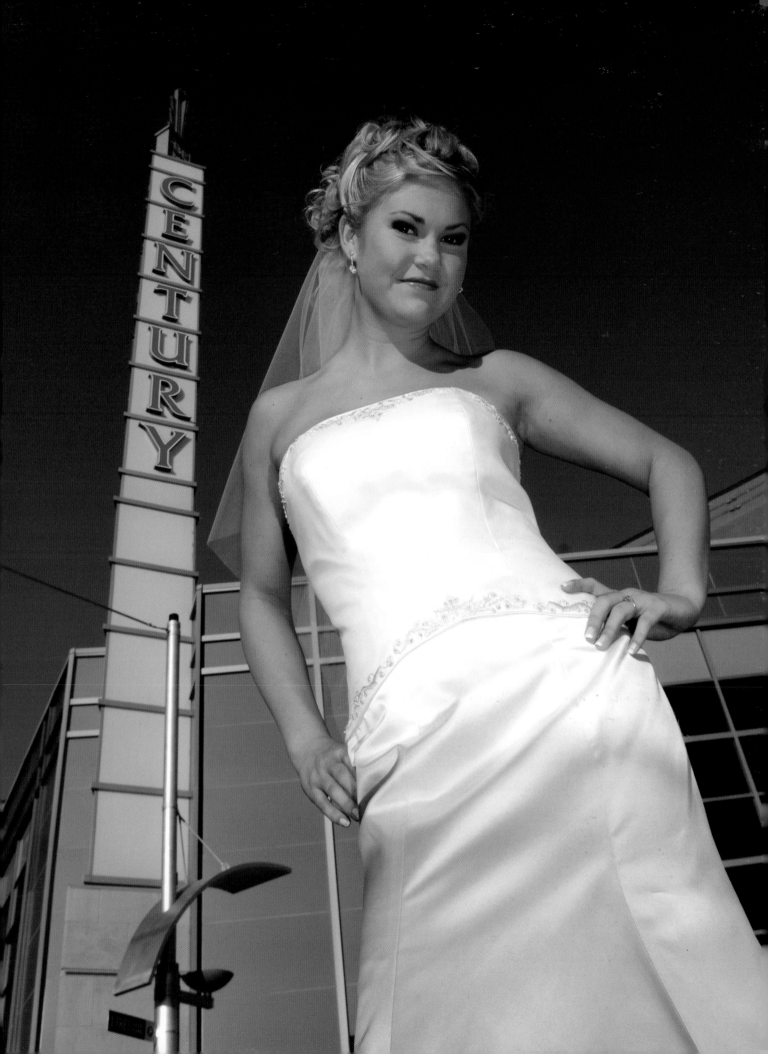

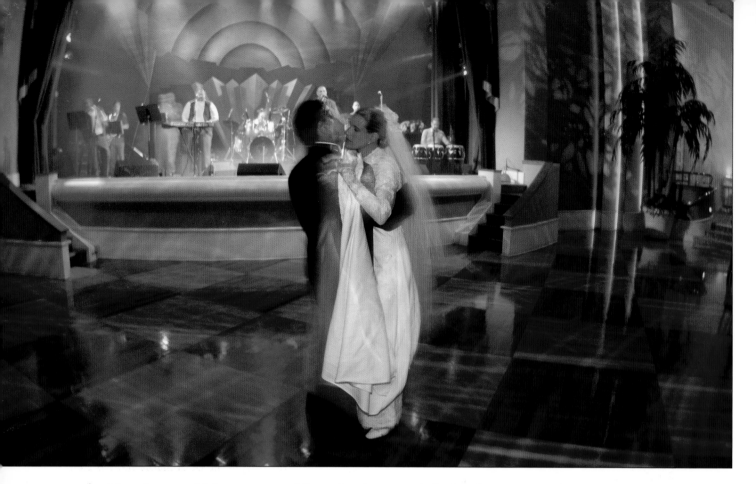

case with us in our vehicle at every wedding—just in case a dark church or foul weather makes it necessary to use them.

When we do use strobes, we use them in conjunction with the ambient light. For instance, if a church's ambient reading is f/8 at $\frac{1}{15}$ second at 400 ISO, we will meter our flashes to f/8. We will make exposures starting at f/8 at $\frac{1}{60}$ second, then f/8 at $\frac{1}{30}$ second, then f/8 at $\frac{1}{15}$ second. Based on these, we will make a determination as to which is most pleasing. The longer you drag the shutter, the more the ambient light will blend in with your photograph. This can be nice to a certain point. Since you are typically shooting in mixed lighting conditions, if you drag the shutter too much your background will appear excessively gold or yellow. Shooting digital, of course, you can immediately make that determination and set your camera accordingly.

I recommend doing these shots on a tripod so you can get away with shutter speeds of $\frac{1}{15}$ second or longer if necessary. If a subject moves, however, they may be blurry. Take enough shots to compensate for this—or, better yet, shoot these at shutter speeds of $\frac{1}{30}$ second or faster. As always, time is on your back, so do all of this testing before your bride and groom are waiting around. For example, when doing portraits after the ceremony, we move our gear to the front of the church

Just a kiss of flash and a long exposure brings out the ambience of the Atlantic Dance Hall at Disney's BoardWalk Inn. (CAMERA: Nikon D1X, ISO: 800, LENS: 16mm, EXPOSURE: 1 second at f/2.8, LIGHTING: on-camera flash at 1 stop less than ambient light, OTHER: tripod)

IF YOU DRAG THE SHUTTER TOO MUCH YOUR BACKGROUND WILL APPEAR EXCESSIVELY GOLD OR YELLOW.

while the guests are still exiting. Once again, do not be rude or obtrusive. Just go along the outer aisles and make your way to the front. The front pews will already be empty, as they usually exit from the front first. Trust me—the church lady and priest will be happy to see that you are hustling. If you plan to use AC strobes at an event, be mindful of your cords. If someone trips or is injured by one, you will be liable and losing your $600 strobe may be the least of your problems.

AVAILABLE LIGHT

Available lighting is more natural than flat, on-camera flash—and usually more flattering, as well. Best of all, available light is extremely easy to carry. Once you embrace it, available light is also an excellent time saver, because you will no longer be weighed down with extra lighting equipment.

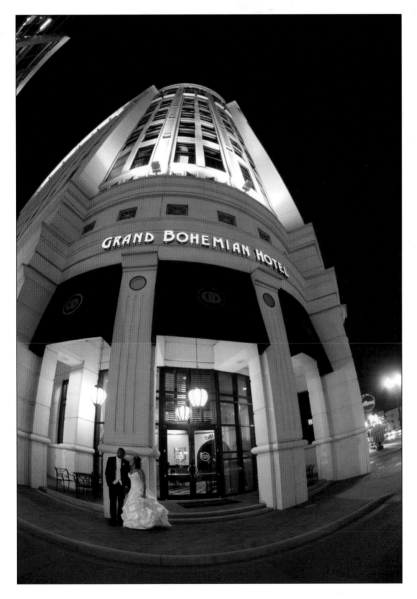

The key to using natural light successfully is training your eye to see it. Good places to find available light include overhangs, situations where light is reflected from a building, window light, and on the shady side of buildings.

Another advantage of available light is that it works very well with the dynamic-range limitations of digital photography. Even though the cameras have progressed immensely, digital image sensors cannot handle the same contrast as film. To combat this, we work in a lot of open shade areas. Today's digital cameras work very well at ISO 800 (or even higher), allowing you to use natural light more easily—you can even employ street lights at night as your only light source.

A steady tripod goes hand in hand with available light. I don't feel comfortable hand-holding shots without a flash for anything longer than a $\frac{1}{100}$ to $\frac{1}{60}$ second shutter speed. Additionally, I like to shoot at f/2.8 for a very limited depth of field—sometimes as little as

With today's digital cameras, night portraits using only available light are easy to create. (CAMERA: Nikon D2Xs, ISO: 800, LENS: 10.5mm fisheye, EXPOSURE: $\frac{1}{6}$ second at f/2.8, OTHER: tripod)

two inches. Consequently, if I move just an iota, the image will be soft. The tripod allows me to drag the shutter as long as I want while restricting camera movement and keeping the image tack sharp. Some photographers hate using tripods, but I disagree. The tripod doesn't slow me; it enables me to capture much more vibrant, dynamic, low-light shots with confidence.

A reflector is also a very helpful tool when using available light—and much easier to carry than a lighting kit. In open shade and window-lit areas we usually employ a large silver reflector to accentuate the light on the subject's face. Typically, I will do a signature head shot of the bride with it. How simple! You have an excellent portfolio shot of the bride in about three minutes.

When possible look for ways to work in open shade. We like to do portraits in these shaded pockets of light for two reasons. First, your subjects will not be squinting. Second, the lighting will have a dynamic range that your camera can capture. Full sun has its place—especially during outdoor ceremonies, for beach shots, and in blue-sky images where the outdoors is part of the scene. Typically, however, if you have a choice of where you are shooting, open shade areas will yield more natural results.

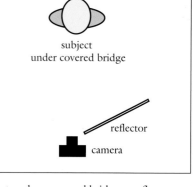

Shot under a covered bridge, a reflector was added to camera right for fill on the bride's face. (**CAMERA:** Nikon D2Xs, **ISO:** 500, **LENS:** 80–200mm at 200mm, **EXPOSURE:** $\frac{1}{200}$ second at f/4)

CONTINUOUS LIGHT

Today's continuous light sources are also well worth mentioning. Continuous lights used to be called hot lights because they were hot to the touch. They still make hot lights, of course, but there is also a new generation of continuous lights that have become popular. These lights do not get hot and they allow you to see exactly what you are getting (unlike when shooting with flash). They come with interchangeable daylight- or tungsten-balanced bulbs, and their power level is adjustable as well.

THERE IS ALSO A NEW GENERATION OF CONTINUOUS LIGHTS THAT HAVE BECOME POPULAR.

We have been looking at the Westcott Spiderlight. It does have some of the pitfalls as the strobes (time to setup, cords, etc.), but it could be a lifesaver in an inclement weather situation or during a wedding with an evening ceremony in which the bride and groom do not wish to see each other before the wedding. It effectively offers you a window-lit type of look, but indoors and after dark. It works in daylight just as well, and we are currently testing this to see if it is a right fit for us. We are also using the Lowell iLight, a small, focusable video-type light equipped with a rheostat.

LIGHT POSITIONS

We have talked about different types of light, now let's talk about different light positions.

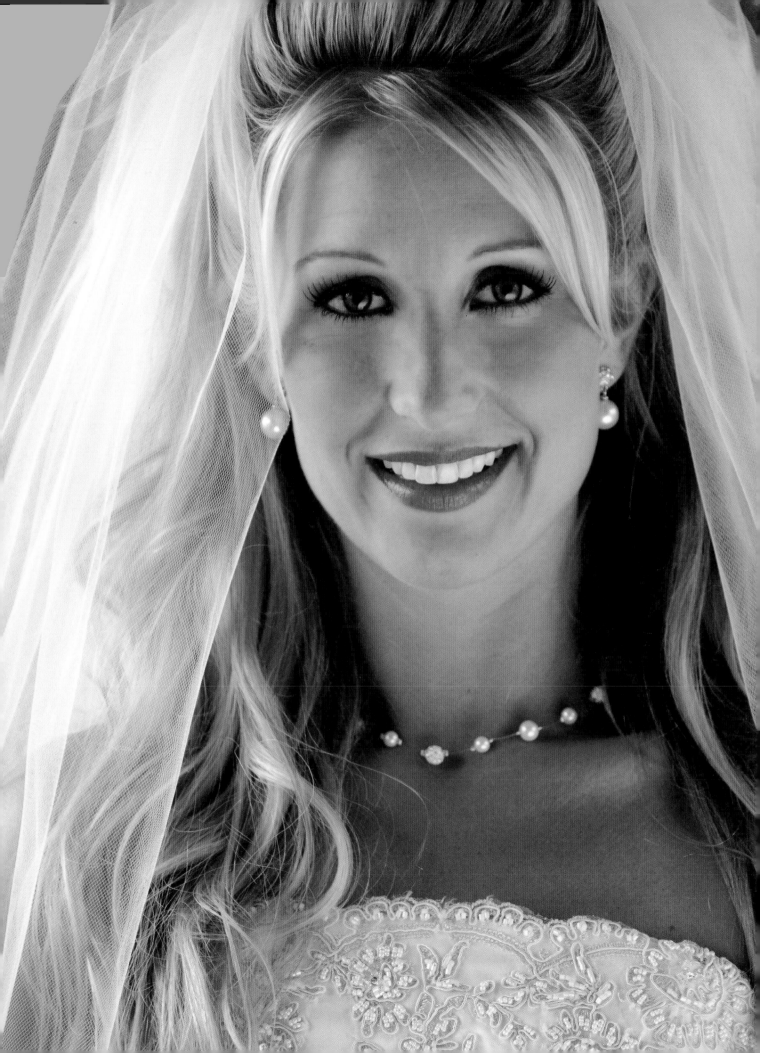

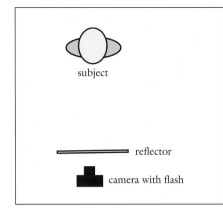

subject

reflector

camera with flash

In this Colorado bride's portrait, the light comes from slightly to camera left. (CAMERA: Nikon D2X, ISO: 100, LENS: 17–55mm f/2.8 at 17mm, LIGHTING: on-camera flash at one stop under the ambient reading; EXPOSURE: ¹⁄₂₅₀ second at f/10)

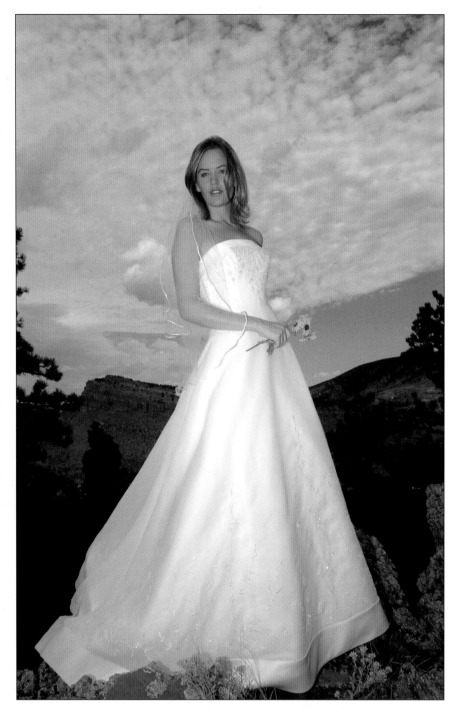

First, it is important to note which side the light should ideally come from. When photographing a bride and groom together, you will usually want the light to come from the bride's side. Typically, the bride is smaller than the groom, so if you did it the opposite way he would block the light falling on her.

Also remember to light the individual bride and groom portraits, whether with strobe or reflector, from the short side. As noted in chapter 10, the camera can add weight to your subjects, which most people definitely don't want to see. We tend to select a higher camera angle to minimize this, but lighting the short side of the face (the side turned away from the camera) will further slim our subjects.

Some of the traditional patterns found in portraiture are also found in wedding photography. The first is the Rembrandt lighting pattern, named after the famous painter. This is denoted by a triangle of light on the shadowed side of the subject's cheek. This is created when the main light source is above face height and at a 90- to 45-degree angle to the subject. The second common pattern is short loop lighting, indicated by a small loop-shaped shadow under the side of the subject's nose opposite of the main light. This is created when the main light is above face height and at less than a 45-degree angle to the subject. The final lighting pattern, called butterfly or clam shell lighting, creates a butterfly-shaped shadow directly under the nose. This is produced when the main light is directly above the subject's face and is generally employed for beauty shots (usually with a fill reflector added below the subject's chin). In the run-and-gun world of wedding photography, we will mostly use variations of the short loop and butterfly lighting techniques with an occasional Rembrandt thrown in.

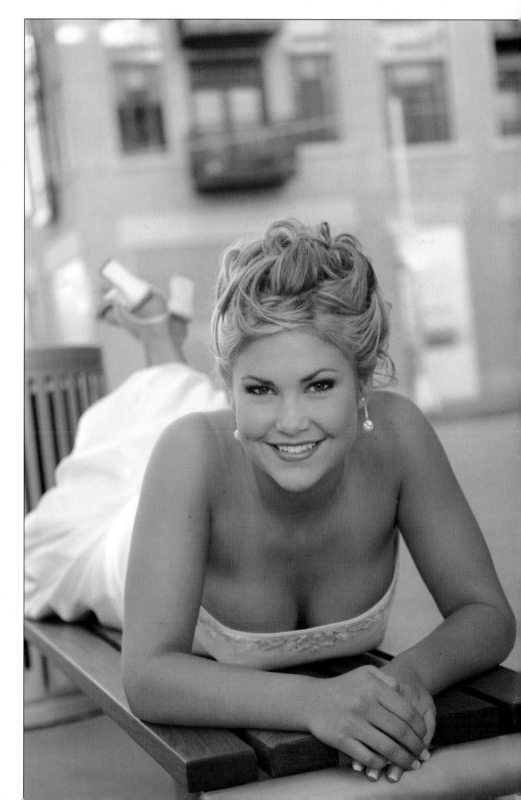

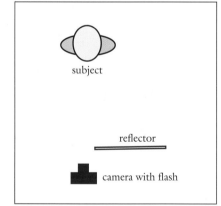

This bridal portrait was shot after the wedding day, so the bride was less concerned about getting her dress dirty. The light was frontal in nature, creating a soft butterfly pattern. (CAMERA: Nikon D2X, ISO: 200, LENS: 50mm f/1.4, EXPOSURE: ¹⁄₂₅₀ second at f/2.8, LIGHTING: on-camera flash at one stop under the ambient reading)

12. File Formats, Exposure, and Focus

WHEN PHOTOGRAPHING A WEDDING we like to keep it simple—but we're not afraid to shoot the heck out of it. Typically, we present sixty images per hour of coverage in our online proofs and in a proof magazine form (essentially bound contact sheets). We usually whittle that down to a total of 250 images that we use in a viewing/sales session. Of course, we shoot many more images than we show. It may be time-consuming to do the editing, but it is better to have what you wanted rather than to have to explain why you don't. Besides, CompactFlash cards are quite economical now, so there's no reason not to bring more than you need just so you'll never be afraid to over-shoot.

FILE FORMATS

When I first started shooting digital, I found working with RAW files to be very cumbersome—but then, I was trained in exposure techniques for slides and transparencies, so I was able to reliably produce great results with JPEG files; I watched my histograms and bracketed. In fact, ninety-five percent of the images in this book were captured in the JPEG-fine format.

TYPICALLY, WE PRESENT SIXTY IMAGES PER HOUR HOUR OF COVERAGE IN OUR ONLINE PROOFS . . .

With the advent of Adobe Lightroom, our studio began shooting in RAW more often. Usually, however, we shot RAW + JPEG and only went back to the RAW file if necessary—we used the RAW file mainly as a safety net. Today, we have started shooting even more events in RAW + JPEG, and we feel that novices would behoove themselves to do so as well. We are still vehement about getting each exposure as perfect as possible, but the benefits of shooting RAW are many. Color correction is a breeze and exposures that in JPEG-fine would be useless can be saved and brought back to life. The sharpening and batch-processing features are also incredible. Shooting in RAW does, of course, have its drawbacks in terms of storage. But this is becoming cheaper and cheaper each day.

Ultimately, RAW processing will give you phenomenal control of your images and push your creativity to the limits. Embracing new workflow tactics is hard, but savvy wedding photographers will keep themselves current and armed with the latest tools. This Adobe Lightroom is no fad and it has brought our imaging to new heights.

EXPOSURE

You know what they say: "Garbage in, garbage out." That is especially true when it comes to digital files. There is no substitute for having a solid exposure to work with.

I am so meticulous about exposure because when I started dabbling in photography, I had a Nikon FE SLR that was given to me by my dad. The meter in the old film SLR did not work so well, so I would line up the arrows like my father taught me . . . but my results were lackluster at best.

Later, another mentor of mine, filmmaker Glen Lau, showed me the recommended exposures that were printed on the film boxes. He also gave me a chart of relative exposures. As it turned out, the film boxes and charts ba-

Left—With digital, there's really no substitute for having a solid exposure to work with. (CAMERA: Nikon D2Xs, ISO: 100, LENS: 10.5mm fisheye, EXPOSURE: ¹⁄₁₆₀ second at f/2.8)

Right—Shooting RAW files will give you great control, but careful exposure techniques can also allow you to obtain excellent results when shooting JPEGs. Here, an emotional bride prepares for her entrance. (CAMERA: Nikon D2Xs, ISO: 800, LENS: 17–55mm at 17mm, EXPOSURE: ¹⁄₁₀₀ second at f/2.8)

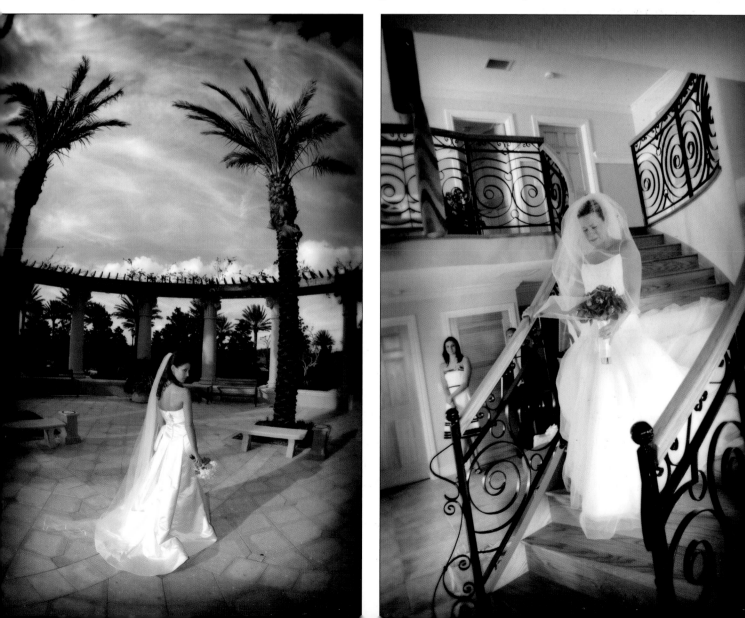

sically gave you the optimal exposures for a variety of different situations. These are:

Bright sunlight on sand or snow . . . .f/16 . . . .$\frac{1}{250}$ second . . . .ISO 100

Bright sun distinct shadows . . . . .f/11 . . . .$\frac{1}{250}$ second . . . .ISO 100

Weak hazy sun . . . . .f/8 . . . .$\frac{1}{250}$ second . . . .ISO 100

Cloudy . . . . .f/5.6 . . . .$\frac{1}{250}$ second . . . .ISO 100

Heavy overcast . . . . .f/5.6 . . . .$\frac{1}{125}$ second . . . .ISO 100

Inside church or restaurant (PM) . . . .f/5.6 . . . . .$\frac{1}{4}$ second . . . .ISO 400

By practicing with these settings, and their relative equivalents, I became something of a human light meter. Nowadays our cameras' meters are incredible, but it will never hurt you to have a working knowledge of the light around you and to have a reference point to start from. Even with all of our technological advances, these basics create a solid foundation to build upon.

LENSES AND FOCUS

We find that digital photography has some issues with focus. In a series of shots, one image is often inexplicably "soft." Overshooting a tad compensates for this, but sharp focus is something we are always very mindful of. There is nothing more disappointing than taking a great image and finding that it is too soft to use.

Left—At the very end of the light, this image was photographed in a close-up view with fill light from a reflector to camera left. A solid understanding of this type of lighting made it easy to get to right exposure in the fading light. (CAMERA: Nikon D2Xs, ISO: 640, LENS: 17–55mm at 55mm, EXPOSURE: $\frac{1}{100}$ second at f/2.8)

Right—The 17–55mm lens tends to be soft at the edges. That makes it a poor choice for group portraits, but an excellent lens for an image like this, where edge sharpness is not a concern. (CAMERA: Nikon D2Xs, ISO: 200, LENS: 17–55mm at 19mm, EXPOSURE: $\frac{1}{200}$ second at f/2.8)

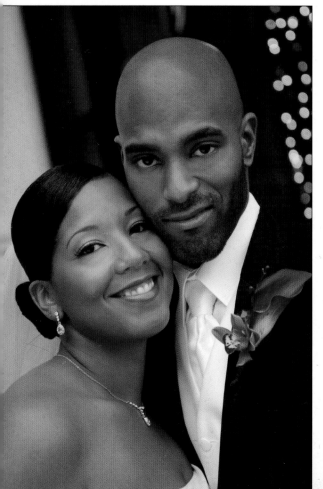

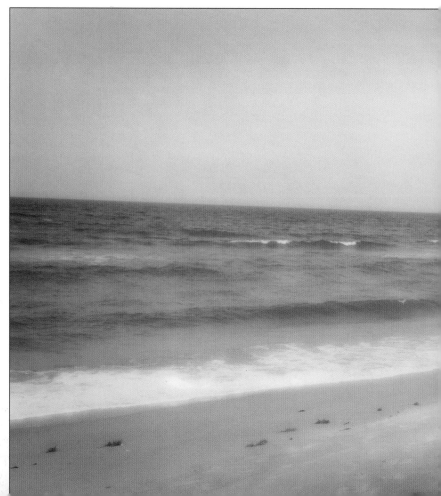

With our Nikon D2X systems, we found that certain lenses were inherently sharper than others. Our favorite was the 50mm f/1.4 lens—an excellent lens for everything from food, to portraits, to weddings. The 10.5mm fisheye is relatively sharp, however you do have to watch the edges. We found that the 17–55mm lens, while versatile, was soft on the edges. This made it a poor candidate for family shots, but it was a favorite for candids where the edge sharpness is not critical. We found that the 17–35mm lens was better for our larger group shots. (We also use the 50mm f/1.4 for groups of four and have a 24mm f/2.8 lens that we use for larger groups.)

AT THE END OF THE DAY, THERE ARE A LOT OF METHODS FOR ACHIEVING SHARP IMAGES.

We tend to shoot things wide open (f/2.8–5.6), because we like the shallow depth of field and it allows us to maximize the ambient lighting. When shooting like this, it is critical to focus precisely. We employ the spot focus method where you hold down the button with the focus on what you want then recompose the shot. That is just what we like to do, though. At the end of the day, there are a lot of methods for achieving sharp images.

As of January 2008, I began shooting with the Nikon D3, a camera I love. The full-frame CMOS sensor is phenomenal, the focus is amazing, and its low-light capabilities are already legendary. With the new camera, our lenses of choice are the 16mm f/2.8 fisheye, the new 24–70mm f/2.8, the 50mm f/1.4, the 85mm f/1.4, and the 80–200mm f/2.8.

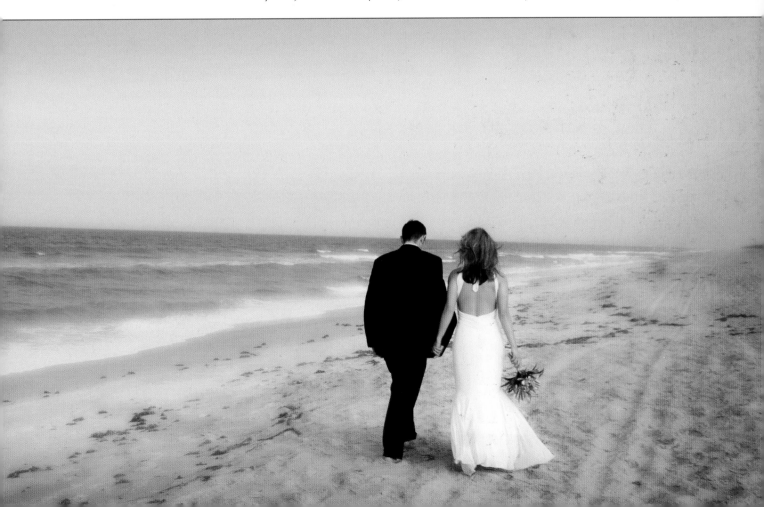

13. Postproduction

CAPTURING A GREAT IMAGE will no longer keep you competitive in today's wedding market. With the advent of digital photography, what you do afterwards is just as important—if not more so. The images we capture must be fiercely edited and polished to perfection.

The savvy photographer has an assortment of tools in his arsenal to help him do this in a timely and aesthetically pleasing manner. Our studio employs many programs and actions that facilitate the editing and polishing of our images. Of course there is Photoshop, but Adobe has also come out with Lightroom, which has helped us with our editing and production of RAW files. We will also discuss Photo Mechanic, Ron Nichols Digital Learning Palettes, Kevin Kubota's and Parker Pfister's actions, and Graphic Authority edges and grunge borders. I'm sure there are many more, but these are the ones that our studio currently uses in conjunction with Photoshop to make our images stand out from the crowd.

> CAPTURING A GREAT IMAGE WILL NO LONGER KEEP YOU COMPETITIVE IN TODAY'S WEDDING MARKET.

ADOBE LIGHTROOM

At the writing of this book, Lightroom is fairly new, but it is already amazing. We learned to use the software by taking a class with Scott Kelby and would highly recommend this. Lightroom is amazing, but getting started can be a little daunting and eight hours with an expert holding your hand will get you off on the right foot. Our staff loves how easily we can now process NEF (Nikon RAW files) and do mass adjustments to JPEGs. Lightroom also comes with built-in actions that are interesting. These make color-correcting a breeze—and the black & white conversions are incredible.

PHOTO MECHANIC

Another editing program we employ is Photo Mechanic. It was originally popular with commercial photographers, but is gaining popularity in other

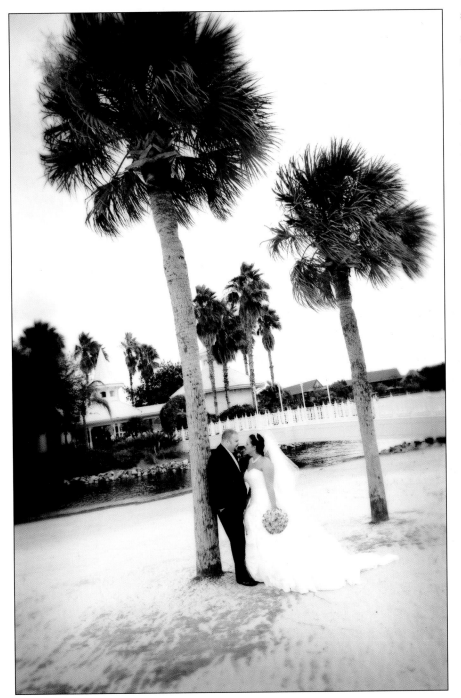

Lightroom offers excellent black & white conversions for your digital files. This image was created right after the ceremony. Rather than photograph the families, we raced outside with the bride and groom to get in about twenty minutes of shooting before a monsoon rolled in. It rained the remainder of our time together. Sometimes you have to know when to punt. (CAMERA: Nikon D2Xs, ISO: 400, LENS: 17–55mm at 17mm, EXPOSURE: $\frac{1}{160}$ second at f/5)

areas of photography because it offers a very fast and effective way to edit and rename your images.

RON NICHOLS PRODUCTION RETOUCHING PALETTE

For our retouching, we often use the Ron Nichols Production Retouching Palette (available at www.ronnichols .com). This program offers a free-floating palette that sends scripting calls into Photoshop to control tools, layers, blending modes, and opacities. It comes with integrated instructional videos that teach you the complete process. This is a great way to give your studio a systematic retouching method. The wonderful thing about it, however, is its amazingly ease of use—great if you are a novice (or if you are training a novice member of your staff). This will free the studio owner to spend more time behind the camera and less in front of the computer. In literally about three minutes, you can effectively retouch an image. We highly recommend it.

KEVIN KUBOTA'S AND PARKER PFISTER'S ACTIONS

Actions, a recorded series of steps in Photoshop, are also very helpful in postproduction. Some come with Photoshop, and you can also make your own, but there are some commercial ones available as well. Two that we use are Kevin Kubota's Artistic Pack I and Artistic Pack II (available at www.kubotaimagetools.com) and Parker Pfister's DDRV (available at www.parkerjddr.com). Both of these actions provide a solid end result with a click of the mouse. The edited image is also layered and, therefore, easily adjustable. Both Parker's and Kubota's actions are real time savers to make above-average images quickly. Some of our stu-

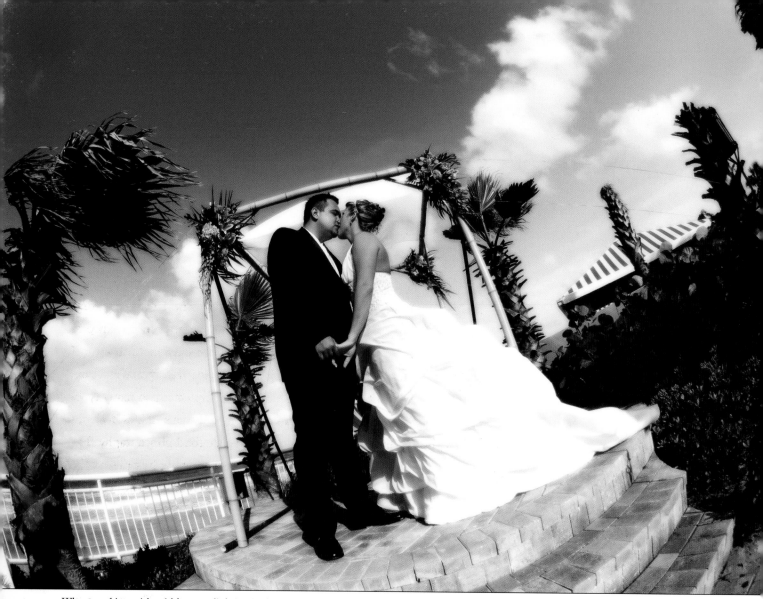

When working with midday sun, lighting is always going to be a challenge. This image was given a little boost in postproduction with Kevin Kubota's Hawaiian Punch action. (**CAMERA:** Nikon D2X, **ISO:** 100, **LENS:** 10.5mm fisheye, **EXPOSURE:** ¹⁄₂₅₀ second at f/10)

dio's favorites from Kevin Kubota are Lord of the Rings, Hawaiian Punch, and all of the cross processes. We also love Parker's Improved Big Run Black-and-White action, as well as all of his toning actions.

GRAPHIC AUTHORITY EDGES

Lastly, we have currently been experimenting with Graphic Authority's collection of grunge edges and contemporary backgrounds. We like the Polaroid transfers, and our brides like some of the scratched looks as well.

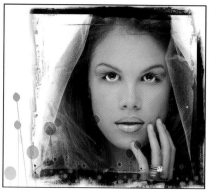

Graphic Authority's edges and backgrounds can add a number of interesting effects.

Finding Your Passion and Style

WE HAVE DISCUSSED MANY THINGS IN THIS BOOK: strategies, gear, time, and techniques. Use all of these to your advantage. Something we have only touched on, however, is passion and style. To really do this job well, you must be passionate about it. I love wedding photography for many reasons. Because I was trained as a generalist, I especially appreciate that it allows me to implement so many types of photography. In a single event, I can go from shooting still lifes, to landscapes, to photojournalism, to portraiture, and even food photography. The wedding is one arena where your every passion for photography can really be unleashed, so if you don't feel passionate about it, you should probably choose another line of work.

Hand-in-hand with passion goes style. If you are to succeed in this business, you must find your own personal style. You must impart something of your personality—even your soul—into every image. Learn the basics, emulate your idols, then set out to find yourself. The end results will communicate much more realness than the cookie-cutter images that are all too often produced at weddings.

This is a process that never ends, so try to surround yourself with greatness, be it music, art, or literature. Consistently look for inspiration. Do not rest on your laurels. This

THIS INDUSTRY IS CONSTANTLY EVOLVING AND YOU WILL BE LEFT BEHIND IF YOU DO NOT EVOLVE WITH IT.

industry is constantly evolving and you will be left behind if you do not evolve with it.

In addition to passion and style, savvy wedding photographers will arm themselves for success with solid skills. There are many tools available to do so. Organizations like Professional Photographers of America (PPA) and Wedding and Portrait Photographers International (WPPI) are valuable resources to beginners and seasoned veterans alike. Both have national conventions every year where photographers can experience camaraderie, print competitions, and a free exchange of ideas and techniques. They also have

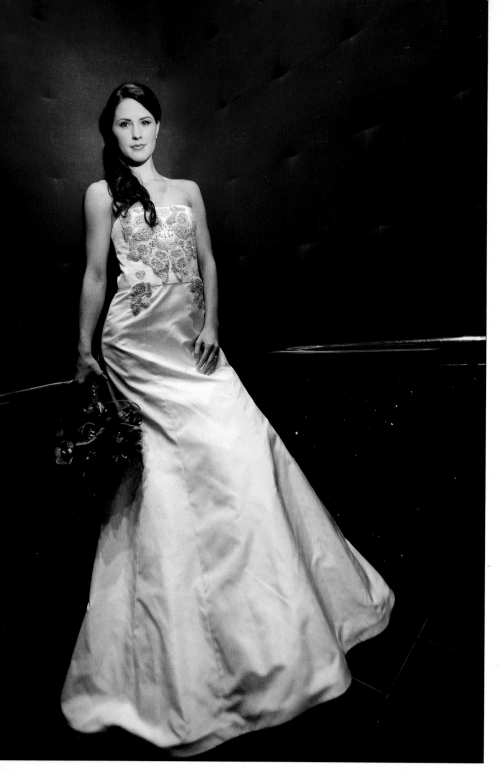

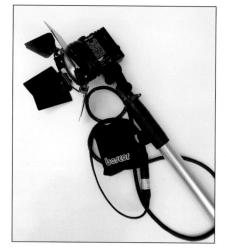

To create this image (left), I took advantage of the wonderful results you can get shooting at high ISO settings on the Nikon D3. This image was actually shot in an elevator, where the 1600 ISO setting allowed me to shoot handheld. A Lowell iLight (above) was also used to accent the bride's face. (**CAMERA:** Nikon D3, **ISO:** 1600, **LENS:** 17–35mm f/2.8 at 17mm)

huge tradeshows where you can get your hands on the latest albums, cameras, and equipment galore.

Both PPA and WPPI also provide business and equipment insurance. As a bonus to its members, PPA also provides wedding indemnification, protecting you against any malpractice lawsuit that may arise. This is a huge asset for the burgeoning wedding photographer. We have a business insurance package through PPA that covers our equipment and studio space. We also have host liability insurance, as we serve wine to clients at our viewing sessions.

There are other groups worth mentioning as well, such as the Digital Wedding Forum (DWF) and www.robgalbraith.com. DWF is an online community where photographers compare work and share ideas. They also have a yearly conference. Robgalbraith.com is an excellent website to get the latest review on that new piece of equipment you may want to buy.

The artistic side of this profession is just one side of the coin. If you want to make a living as a photographer, you need to embrace the business side of it as well. Try not to go overboard with spending in the beginning. I worked out of the loft I lived in when I first left Walt Disney World, and I can promise you that having no overhead is a good thing! Take it slow and build a solid infrastructure. There is a lot more to being a successful wedding photographer than taking great images. Networking, marketing, and business plans all come into play (maybe these should be the subject of my next book!).

Wedding photography may not be open heart surgery, but clients take it just as seriously. Be responsible and embrace your craft to the best of your ability. Always strive to exceed your client's expectations. After all, who doesn't like to get the thirteenth donut in the baker's dozen? That's how we roll at Damon Tucci Studios.

Good Luck,
Damon

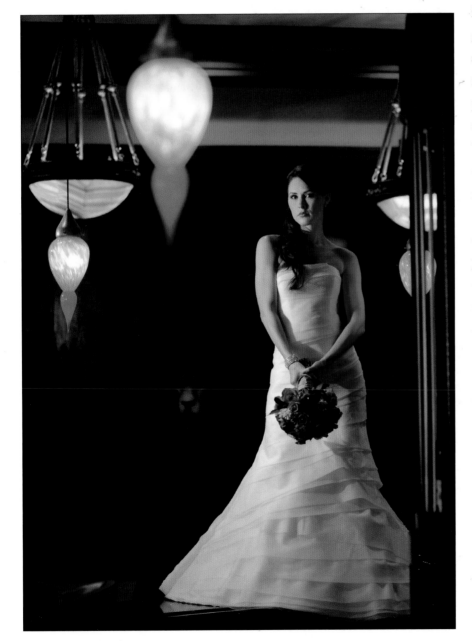

For this bridal portrait, natural light was combined with illumination from a Lowell iLight, which provided directional lighting from camera left. (CAMERA: Nikon D3, ISO: 800, LENS: 80–200mm f/2.8 at 92mm, EXPOSURE: 1/40 second at f/2.8)

Index

A

ACDSee, 84
Adobe Lightroom, 44, 84
Anticipating events, 11, 92–94
Assistant, working with, 39–41,
    50–52, 94–95
Available light, using, 88–91, 111–12

B

Backgrounds, 7–8, 62–64
Bouquet toss, 81–82
Bridal portraits, 12, 15, 28–35,
    59–72
Bride and groom, portraits of,
    59–72

C

Cake, 70, 77
Cake cutting, 80–81
Camera angle, 96–98
Ceremony, 36–53
    communion, 46
    exposure, 41–43
    first kiss, 46
    giving bride away, 44
    Hindu weddings, 46–48
    Jewish weddings, 46, 48
    outdoor, 48–53
    positioning yourself, 39–41,
        50–52
    ring exchange, 45–46
    second photographer, role of,
        39–41, 50–52
    unity candle, 46
    venue rules, 36–40
    white balance, 43–44

Communion, 46
Consultation, 13–18
    educating client, 15–18
    understanding client's goals, 13
    wedding locations, 14
    wedding timeline, 14
Corbell, Tony, 64, 98

D

Detail shots, 15
Digital Wedding Forum (DWF), 125

E

Emergencies, being prepared for, 18
Equipment, 19–21, 74, 84, 108–15,
    118–19
    backup, 20–21
    bags for, 20–21
    cameras, 20, 119
    cases for, 20
    checklist, 19
    excessive, 21
    inventory before leaving event, 84
    lenses, 20, 118–19
    lighting, 108–15
    light stands, 20
    Lowell iLight, 112
    packing, 19–21
    Quantum Turbo SC, 74
    securing, 21
    tripods, 20
    Westcott Spiderlight, 112
Exit shots, 83
Exposure, 41–43, 48–53, 117–18
    indoor ceremonies, 41–43
    outdoor ceremonies, 48–53

F

Family portraits, 12, 15–17, 28–35,
    54–58, 105–6
    before the ceremony, 28–35
    discussing at consultation, 12,
        15–17
    efficiency, 55–56
    large groups, 57–58
    lighting, 56–57
    maintaining control, 58
    posing, 105–6
File formats, 44, 116–17
First dance, 74–75
First kiss, 46
Flash, 38, 53, 108–11
    fill, 53
    techniques, 108–11
    use of during ceremony, 38
Formal portraits, *see* Posed portraits

G

Garter toss, 81–82
Gear, *see* Equipment
Getting ready, bride, 22–35, 88
    dressing, 26–28
    emotional brides, 25
    listening, importance of, 24, 88
    names, learning, 24
    second shooter, 26–28
    what to shoot, 22
Goals, setting, 8
Groom portraits, 12, 16, 35, 59–72

H

Hindu weddings, 46–48

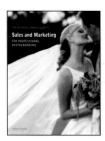
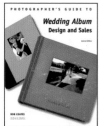
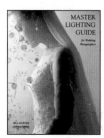
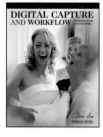
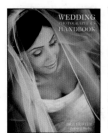
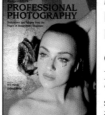
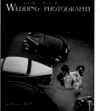